# Fencing

## Steps to Success

**Elaine Cheris**
Cheyenne Fencing and Modern Pentathlon Center

**Human Kinetics**

**Library of Congress Cataloging-in-Publication Data**

Cheris, Elaine.
    Fencing: steps to success / Elaine Cheris.
        p.     cm. -- (Steps to success activity series)
    ISBN 0-87322-972-X
    1. Fencing.    I. Title.    II. Series.
    GV1147 .C44   2001
    796.86--dc21                                          2001039983

ISBN: 978-0-87322-972-2

**Managing Editor:** Melinda Graham; **Assistant Editor:** John Wentworth; **Copyeditor:** Don Amerman; **Proofreader:** Scott Weckerly; **Graphic Designer:** Keith Blomberg; **Cover Designer:** Jack W. Davis; **Cover Photographer:** Tom Roberts; **Illustrator:** John Hatton; **Printer:** Total Printing Systems

Instructional Designer for the Steps to Success Activity Series: Joan N. Vickers, EdD, University of Calgary, Calgary, Alberta, Canada

Human Kinetics books are available at special discounts for bulk purchase. Special editions or book excerpts can also be created to specification. For details, contact the Special Sales Manager at Human Kinetics.

Printed in the United States of America            20      19      18      17      16      15

The paper in this book is certified under a sustainable forestry program.

**Human Kinetics**
Website: www.HumanKinetics.com

*United States:* Human Kinetics
P.O. Box 5076
Champaign, IL 61825-5076
800-747-4457
e-mail: humank@hkusa.com

*Canada:* Human Kinetics
475 Devonshire Road Unit 100
Windsor, ON N8Y 2L5
800-465-7301 (in Canada only)
e-mail: info@hkcanada.com

*Europe:* Human Kinetics
107 Bradford Road
Stanningley
 Leeds LS28 6AT, United Kingdom
+44 (0) 113 255 5665
e-mail: hk@hkeurope.com

*Australia:* Human Kinetics
57A Price Avenue
Lower Mitcham, South Australia 5062
08 8372 0999
e-mail: info@hkaustralia.com

*New Zealand:* Human Kinetics
P.O. Box 80
Torrens Park, South Australia 5062
0800 222 062
e-mail: info@hknewzealand.com

# CONTENTS

# PREFACE

Fencing is not for everyone, but anyone can fence. The advantage fencing has over most other sports is that fencing is not physically selective. Your size, shape, or weight does not determine your fencing future. Your future in fencing comes from inside. Your capacity for work and your desire are the determining factors. People who fence are people who like to make decisions for themselves rather than having decisions made for them. Fencing is an intensive physical replica of a computer game in which the mind must race quickly to meet unforeseen challenges.

Fencing is also physically challenging and improves the conditioning of the fencer as he or she learns skill and technique. Fencing allows participants to challenge their fitness and conditioning levels at a comfortable level without overdoing. The mind and body adjust while fencing. If legs or arms begin to tire, the fencer moves automatically to another aspect of the fencing game. The more you fence, the better you will learn to compensate for physical fatigue through changing the style of play. The same adaptation also occurs when part of your game just isn't working on a particular day. In fencing, nothing you do will work every day on every opponent you face, so you'll be adjusting constantly.

Fencing has been influenced by technology. In the modern era fencing has progressed from a static form of eloquent style to a dynamic form of efficient movements. With electronic scoring, we no longer depend on judges to see and hear our touches, which means we can move much quicker, knowing all our touches will be detected by the scoring system. Emphasis was once on style in order to impress the judges; now emphasis is on scoring. Today's fencing match is much faster than yesterday's and much more efficient. Rather than five judges watching a match from different positions, a2 single referee calls penalties and analyzes actions to determine priorities.

Fencing is changing in other ways as well. Years ago, great sums of money were paid to coaches who could devise unique new ways of winning duels. After a great influx of new moves, the sport locked into a system that remained static for hundreds of years and which only now is returning to the days of development and growth. No longer is there one right way to fence or to perform a particular movement. Fencers are doing what's necessary to score, and coaches are analyzing and developing new actions and variations. Since the opening of the gates to Eastern Europe, coaches and fencers now travel easily from country to country and continent to continent. New ideas and concepts quickly circulate through the world. As fencers continue to prove that many different approaches and styles can produce success, more coaches are accepting methods that years ago they would have never considered. With the changing of winning styles and approaches to fencing, coaches must help students find solutions for a variety of attacks and defenses.

I decided to write this book to illustrate the metamorphosis that the training of a fencer is undergoing. I'll be teaching ways in which actions can be taken and the thoughts behind them. The style will be dynamic. As I intend the book to be used by fencers and coaches as a foundation upon which to develop their own styles, you'll find few "rules" to follow here. Learn and practice the steps included here, and then experiment, making minor modifications to suit your style. My objective is make you comfortable with the sport and feel confident of your ability to play to win. Many years of training and working with progressive coaches are necessary to become a champion.

Although fencing is practiced in three disciplines—foil, epee, and saber—in this book I cover only foil and epee, since the two are so similar. Unless I mention one or the other weapon specifically, all my comments relate to both. All skill descriptions and illustrations are for right-handers, so left-handers will need to reverse them. (Sorry, lefties, but don't feel bad—once you learn the sport, you'll find you have a distinct advantage in being the minority. You're more accustomed to their look than they are to yours.)

We'll begin by teaching you the basic skills to practice on your own, first without a weapon and then by adding the foil or epee. After you have reached a sufficient level, I'll add partner and opponent drills to simulate the bouting that puts all the physical and mental skills together. Finally, I'll guide you through an actual bout.

Good luck and have fun!

# THE STEPS TO SUCCESS STAIRCASE

Get ready to climb a staircase—one that will lead you to become an accomplished fencer. You can't leap to the top; you get there by climbing one step at a time.

Each of the nine steps you will take is an easy transition from the one before. The first few steps of the staircase provide a solid foundation of basic skills and ideas. As you progress, you'll learn how to develop these skills and ideas to maneuver your opponent around the floor. As you near the top of the staircase, you'll become more confident in your ability to challenge higher-level fencers in competition or just for fun.

Read this section, as well as the "History of Fencing," for an orientation and help with setting up your practice sessions around the steps.

Follow the same sequence each step (chapter) of the way:

1. Read the explanations of what the step covers, why the step is important, and how to execute or perform the step's focus, which may be on basic skills, ideas, tactics, or a combination of the three.

2. Follow the numbered illustrations showing exactly how to position your body to execute each basic skill. Each skill has three general parts: preparation (getting into a starting position), execution (performing the skill that is the focus of the step), and follow-through (reaching a finishing position or following through to starting position).

3. Look over the common errors that may occur and the recommendations for how to correct them.

4. The drills help you improve your skills through repetition and purposeful practice. Read the directions and the Success Goal for each drill. Practice accordingly and record you scores. Compare your score with the Success Goal for the drill. You need to meet the Success Goal of each drill before moving on to the practice for the next one because the drills are arranged in an easy-to-difficult progression. This sequence is designed to help you achieve continual success.

5. When you can reach all the Success Goals for one step, you are ready for a qualified observer—such as your teacher, coach, or trained partner—to evaluate your basic skill technique against the Keys to Success checklist. This is a qualitative or subjective evaluation of your basic technique for form, because using correct form can enhance your performance.

6. Repeat these procedures for each of the nine Steps to Success. Then rate yourself according to the directions in the "Rating Your Progress" section.

Good luck on your step-by-step journey to developing your fencing skills, building confidence, experiencing success, and having fun!

# HISTORY OF FENCING

Fencing, both as a sport and a form of warfare, has been in existence for 4,000 years. An early sporting match was captured in a relief carving in the temple of Madinet-Habu at Luxor, Egypt. The weapons are shown to have blunted tips, and the fencers are wearing masks. The carving also shows the spectators, officials, and a scorekeeper.

During the Middle Ages, the swords grew into heavy and somewhat clumsy weapons to counter the use of armor and bludgeon one's opponent into submission, rather than thrusting the point of the weapon. The invention of gun powder altered the form of warfare. It not only did away with armored soldiers, but it also created the artistry of the sword. Without armor to hamper one's own movements, as well as giving one's opponent a protective shell, the sword became a thrusting weapon, and the skilled use of the sword became extremely important. The swords became lighter, and the actions became faster.

Guilds of fencing masters developed throughout Europe, where fighting with the sword was studied and taught. These moves were not always the pure fencing maneuvers of today's sport but included wrestling moves as well. Secrets of the bout were developed in different schools and sprung upon others in actual fights. After hundreds of years and the advent of video replay, there are very few, if any, bout secrets in existence. It is timing, distance, and technique rather than a surprising new move that bring victory in today's combat.

The Italian school first developed the effective use of the point of the weapon and introduced the rapier. With the development of more refined footwork, including the lunge, the wrestling and body contact diminished. Since the rapier was a rather long weapon, which was unwieldy at closer quarters, the left hand used a dagger, which provided much of the defense while the rapier was going for the hit.

In the seventeenth century, the French developed the shorter court sword, which every gentleman wore, ready to defend his or his lady's honor at the slightest provocation. Every man of breeding learned fencing. It was the true mark of a gentleman.

The court sword replaced the rapier and in so doing also made the dagger obsolete because the shorter court sword could be controlled more easily both offensively and defensively. However, the fencing at closer quarters and the swifter movements resulted in more eye injuries, and it was a rare fencing master that reached his death with both eyes still sighted. Rules were developed to cut down on the practice injuries.

The first rules required fencers to make hits only on the right breast, and they granted the fencer who first began an attack the power to complete it unless he was parried. Although the Egyptians used masks 4,000 years ago, masks were not in general use until the end of the eighteenth century.

The invention of the mask by La Boessiere made even more complex movements possible without great danger of injury. The "conversations" of the swords came to be the norm of the sport. It could have become a mere jumble of blades flailing, but rules and conventions have continued to develop to this day to keep the sport fast and interesting both for the fencer and the spectator alike.

In 1896 fencing was one of the original sports in the Olympics and has remained there ever since. It also has another place in the Olympics as a part of the modern pentathlon, which combines fencing with riding, shooting, running, and swimming. During the late nineteenth century and early twentieth century the judging was done by a jury of five with the president describing the action and the judges and the president voting on whether a hit was properly made and arrived on the valid target area. Uniforms had to be all white to assist the judges in determining whether a hit was made. In epee the tip of the weapon carried a drop of red dye to assist the judges in seeing the hit, since the target in epee is the whole body. Epee, then foil, and finally saber are now electronically scored. The uniforms once again are starting to have the color and flair of the French musketeers, although they have many modern safety features, including the use of kevlar to prevent the puncture of a broken blade through the uniform.

Today fencing is a dynamic sport calling for years of training. It requires a keen eye, a supple mind, and a fit body. It is also a sport for all ages. Youngsters at 6 are sporting their swords in clubs throughout the country, and Olympic status can be gained at 16 or 56. All it takes is practice and desire.

# STEP 1

# ON GUARD STANCE AND MOBILITY:
## MOVING ON THE STRIP

The first steps in becoming a fencer are learning a balanced on guard position, how to move smoothly and rapidly in either direction, and how to make crisp changes in direction without any loss of balance. The purpose of these steps is not to learn all of the intricate footwork that Olympians exhibit but to learn basic mobility so that you will be capable of learning the more complex skills later.

Footwork has many variations. In this step we will teach the salute, on guard position, advance, retreat, and bounce. These are the basic tools you will need to begin to defend your space. The time spent practicing these skills without having a weapon in your hand to distract you will pay dividends later when your focus is shifted to "reading" your opponent and making the appropriate offensive or defensive moves. Your mobility on the strip (on guard, advance, retreat, and bounce) has to become as second nature as walking or running.

## Why Is the Salute Important?

One of the oldest traditions in sport, the salute acknowledges respect for the opponent as a worthy competitor. The gesture signals an understanding between opponents: Within the confines of the rules of this great and classic sport, may the best fencer win.

Before and after drilling, training, bouting, or receiving a lesson, fencers salute their opponents or instructors. The salute is required all over the world, with no exceptions to the rule. While some fencers might create their own style, the salute always involves bringing the hand holding the weapon to the chin.

During your salute, stand erect, tall, and proud. Stand half facing your opponent, holding your mask in your unarmed hand and your sword extended in the direction of your opponent but toward the floor, the point a few inches from the ground (diagram 1a). Bring the guard (the part of the sword that protects your hand from the opponent's blade) close to your chin, pointing the sword upward (diagram 1b). Then return the sword to the original position (diagram 1c). The weapon must never touch the ground during the salute.

After the bout, follow your salute with a good, strong handshake. No wet, limp, disrespectful shakes allowed! Maybe you won and maybe you lost, but your handshake should stay the same. If you have won, don't get too excited, as this might be taken as disrespect by the opponent. If you have lost, hold your head high and act as if you have won and say "good bout." Never show anger to your opponent or partner, as such emotion only distracts you from your purpose and delays progress. Your purpose is to learn as much as you can as quickly as you can and apply what you learn under the most stressful situations. Stay mentally, physically, and emotionally disciplined, always under control.

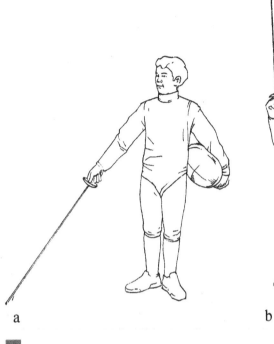  

a              b        c

**Diagram 1**    The salute

## Why Are the On Guard Stance and Mobility Important?

The on guard position is an empowering ready position that allows for dynamic offensive and defensive maneuvers. The on guard is a sideways position that makes you a more difficult target to hit, as well as allowing you a longer reach. Your ability to move is critical in fencing because the most dangerous ground in fencing is that on which you are standing. To minimize this danger you must keep moving and changing the distance between your opponent and you. Your intention is to have complete balance and fluid mobility on the strip, including the ability to change direction any time the situation dictates. This will increase your ability to control the space in the same way that Michael Jordan did on a basketball court. His ability to change direction and move with great speed causes the person guarding him to give him more space in order not to be left in the dust. So too in fencing your mobility permits you to control the distance between your opponent and you.

This is one of the key elements of bouting. Good footwork is the key to becoming a superior fencer; if your opponent cannot catch you, he cannot hit you. With good footwork you can easily escape your opponent and can just as easily catch your opponent.

## How to Execute the On Guard Position

You can begin to learn your on guard position anywhere. Probably the best place to start is in front of a full-length mirror where you can see yourself as your opponent would. Start by facing the mirror, standing erect with your arms and shoulders relaxed, hands on hips. Next, move your left foot so that your heel is directly behind the right heel and at a 90-degree angle, making an "L" with your feet.

Step out with your dominant/front foot so that the distance between your heels is approximately equal to the width of your shoulders or about 1 1/2 times the length of your foot. Bend your knees and position them over the laces of your shoes. Press out with your knees; do not allow them to collapse inward. Your weight should be distributed evenly on the balls of your feet with your hips rotated slightly toward your front foot (the "dominant side"). Your head should be held erect and facing directly toward the mirror. Figure 1.1a shows the epee on guard position; b shows on guard for foil.

Your on guard position should empower you, making you feel ready to move forward or backward with equal control and balance. The on guard stance is very similar to the surfing stance, where the person also must be in perfect balance at all times. Extend your front arm in the same direction as front foot and thigh. Your arm should be straight out from your shoulder, parallel to the floor, with your fingers extended and thumb pointing up at 1 o'clock. Drop your elbow down, bending your arm. Keep your forearm parallel to the floor and the wrist straight. Your forearm should be slightly up from parallel for foil and parallel to the floor for epee. Your other arm (back arm) should be held in a graceful arc over your shoulder, similar to the ballet position. Figure 1.1c shows the arm position for epee and d shows it for foil.

There are a few biomechanical differences between foil and epee on guard positions. As shown in the following illustration, in foil the feet are slightly wider apart, the knee bend is greater, the upper body is pressed forward more in the direction of the opponent, and the arm is bent more.

FIGURE 1.1 **KEYS TO SUCCESS**

# ON GUARD

a                    b                    c        d

1. Feet at 90-degree angle, heels in a line, shoulder width apart, knees flexed __
2. Front wrist, elbow, shoulder, hip, knee, and foot in the same vertical plane ____

3. Rear arm in an arc over your rear shoulder __
4. Shoulders and hips level ___

# Why Are the Advance, Retreat, and Bounce Important?

When you are able to reach your opponent with the tip of your weapon, you are said to be in "scoring distance." At least half of the touches in a bout are scored because a fencer was able to move forward toward the opponent to get within distance or because he failed to move backward to get out of distance when the opponent was moving toward him. If you can hit your opponent with an advance you are in "advance distance," with a lunge you are in lunge distance, and so on. It is important to be able to use the advance, retreat, and bounce to get in or out of distance during the bout.

The retreat and the advance are used in combination. You can use the advance and retreat in a variety of tactical ways by changing the length or tempo (rhythm) of your movement so your opponent loses her tempo and distance. This gives you a greater opportunity to score, either on her untimely attack (giving you a better opportunity to defend yourself and score), or on your precisely timed attack.

Bouncing is an aerobic, very dynamic way of moving forward and backward. Since bouncing uses an extreme amount of energy you may want to use it sparingly until your conditioning catches up to your skill level. Bouncing keeps you in a constant state of readiness, as well as masking your intentions. You can change direction and tempo in an instant. It also assists your explosiveness and helps you to react quickly to an opponent's actions. Your body position remains the same as in the on guard. Bouncing is also an excellent way to condition your fencing muscles rapidly.

When you begin fencing with another person, you may want to use advances and retreats to conserve energy and maintain long distance. Then use bouncing when the intensity builds and your opponent and you enter the danger zone where touches are scored.

## Advance

An advance is a step forward from an on guard position in the direction of your opponent. It helps you maneuver closer to your opponent so that you will be able to reach him with the tip of your weapon either directly or with the use of the additional footwork that you will learn in Step 3, Lunge and Recovery.

## How to Advance

From the on guard position (figure 1.2a), move your front foot forward by lifting the toe first and taking a small step forward (figure 1.2b), followed immediately by your rear foot. Move both feet the same distance. You need to move the rear foot quickly and firmly, keeping both knees flexed and pressed outward during the entire action (figure 1.2c). Think and feel like you are moving your rear foot twice as fast and half the distance as you are moving the front, even though you actually will be moving your feet exactly the same distance. The front foot cannot make another move until the rear foot is positioned. Your head should not bob up and down but remain at the same level parallel to the floor during an advance.

FIGURE
1.2
**KEYS TO SUCCESS**

# ADVANCE

a

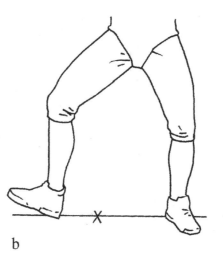
b

c

## Preparation

1. Position yourself in the on guard position____

## Execution

1. Step forward with the front foot, lifting the toe first, followed immediately by the back foot ____
2. Do not lift your feet more than 1 inch (10 cm) above the floor ____

3. Keep your toes and knee of front leg pointed forward____
4. Keep your toes and knee of rear leg pointed at a 90-degree angle to the direction of the advance____

## Retreat

The retreat is needed to maintain correct distance with your opponent. It is used to repair the distance when you are too close to defend against your opponent's delivery of a hit. You also can use retreats to get your opponent to come forward, creating opportunities for you to score.

## How to Retreat

In the retreat you first move your rear foot backward, then move your front foot backward the same distance, as quickly as possible. Maintain a constant distance of about shoulder width between your feet. You will feel like you are moving your front foot half the distance your rear foot moves and twice as fast, even though you actually will be moving your feet the same distance. Figures 1.3a-c show the progression of the retreat.

**FIGURE 1.3**  **KEYS TO SUCCESS**

# RETREAT

### Preparation

1. Balanced on guard position____

a          b          c

### Execution

1. Move your rear foot back first, then immediately move the front foot back____
2. Keep your feet within 1 inch (10 cm) of the floor____

3. Retreat on the balls of your feet____
4. Flex knees and press them outward, keeping your knees over your shoelaces ____

## How to Bounce

The bounce is simply a slight spring done by the feet and arches with a minimum amount of movement in the knees. The easiest way to learn the bounce is to jump rope, just clearing the floor with your feet. Start in the on guard position and bounce up and down, keeping your knees bent to the same degree (figure 1.4a). Spring from your feet, not your knees. Both feet leave the floor at the same time and land on the floor at the same time (figure 1.4b). Keep center of gravity between your feet.

**FIGURE 1.4**    **KEYS TO SUCCESS**

# BOUNCING

a

b

### Preparation

1. Balanced on guard position____

### Execution

1. Stay on the balls of your feet____
2. Keep knees bent and spring from the feet____
3. Feet leave the floor at the same time____
4. Feet land on the floor at the same time____

## How to Bounce Forward

The bounce forward not only moves you toward your opponent with greater speed than the advance, it also hides your intentions from your opponent. Moves from the bounce are very deceptive and make you appear faster than you really are. Because of the movement of the bounce it is difficult for your opponent to recognize exactly when your real action begins.

As you bounce forward, both feet leave the floor at the same time. Move in a forward motion, not upward. The speed and distance that each bounce forward travels depends on the action of the opponent and your intent. You go forward as fast and as far as needed to arrive at the right distance to permit you to hit your opponent. However, the action should cover between 6 to 8 inches (15–20 cm). Going much farther in one bounce would make you vulnerable either because you were in the air too long or because you would not be in a balanced position. The forward bounce is used in combination with the bounce back to maintain appropriate distance between fencers.

Although the terminology is called bouncing, it is truly a slight forward and backward springing motion, parallel to the ground and not vertical. Unlike the advance the head does move up and down to a small degree. Minimize the up and down movement as much as possible.

## How to Bounce Backward

The bounce backward supplements the retreat and allows you to spring away from your opponent. Remember, however, that the objective is not merely to avoid your opponent's touch, but to put yourself at the appropriate distance for you to score.

In the bounce backward, you start in the on guard position (figure 1.5a) and both feet again leave the ground at the same time (figure 1.5b). The speed and distance that each bounce back covers depends on the action of the opponent and your intent or purpose. You should go back as fast and as far as needed to avoid being hit, as well as to arrive at the right distance to permit you to begin an offensive response to your opponent's action. The bounce backward is used in combination with the bounce forward to maintain appropriate distance with your opponent.

| FIGURE 1.5 | KEYS TO SUCCESS |

# BOUNCING FORWARD AND BACKWARD

a

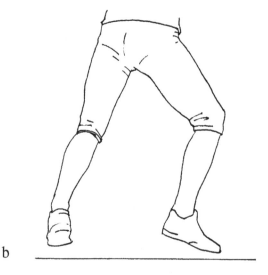

b

### Preparation

1. Balanced on guard position___

### Execution

1. Keep knees bent all the time you are bouncing___
2. Stay on the balls of your feet___
3. Feet leave the floor at the same time with a forward or backward push___
4. Feet land on the floor at the same time with a very slight cushioning at the knees___
5. Land in a balanced position, ready to move in either direction___

## SUCCESS STOPPERS

It is not enough merely to recognize a problem with the on guard stance—you must be able to make a correction to solve a problem. Here are some common flaws of the on guard position and ways to fix them.

The major errors in the advance and retreat occur when you permit the weight to shift and the body to sway from foot to foot. This gives a signal to your opponent of your movement. If you cover short amounts of ground quickly with crisp steps without dragging your feet, you can keep your problems and errors to a minimum. Move your feet so that if you were viewed from the waist up it would appear as though you were on wheels. Don't pause between steps when changing direction. Keep your feet on the floor as much as possible; quick, small steps are most advantageous. Keep weight centered between your feet.

| Error | Correction |
|---|---|
| **On Guard Stance** | |
| 1. Stand with legs straight. | 1. Flex knees. Press rear hip down. |
| 2. Feel out of balance or with more weight on one foot. | 2. From the on guard position, as a drill only, straighten your knees and rise onto your toes and lower yourself back into the on guard position several times to feel your balanced position. You may also bounce lightly to find your balanced position. |
| 3. Knees collapse inward. | 3. Rotate hips slightly forward until front knee is over shoelaces. Press knees outward. |
| 4. Feel that the position is causing your body to be stiff or tense. | 4. You probably are standing too much in profile, causing tension in your shoulder and hips. Turn your hips and shoulders slightly forward to relieve stressed areas. |
| **Advance and Retreat** | |
| 1. Advance by moving the rear foot first. | 1. Advances always start with the front foot. |
| 2. Begin retreat with the front foot first. | 2. Retreats always start with the rear foot. |
| 3. Drag trailing foot or front heel. | 3. Move trailing foot quickly and crisply, lifting it slightly. Take smaller steps. |
| 4. Body shifts forward or backward with advance or retreat. | 4. Body position remains steady and center of gravity does not shift. |
| **Bouncing** | |
| 1. Straighten the knees, gaining too much height. | 1. Bounce primarily with your feet and ankles. Keep knees always bent and feet close to the floor. |
| 2. Shift weight forward or backward. | 2. Keep weight evenly distributed between your feet. Do not move your head; keep chin steady. |
| 3. Toeing in. | 3. Keep front knee and toes in a straight line toward the opponent. |

## ON GUARD STANCE AND MOBILITY

# DRILLS

The purpose of these drills is to make permanent muscle memory of the correct on guard position so you will be able to keep this position while moving forward or backward rapidly. These drills also begin to teach your body to function and respond correctly to the opponent while your mind is focused on your opponent and actions necessary to score.

For the following drills you will need a mirror with an open space of at least five meters (16.4 feet), longer if possible, and a partner, if one is available. You will need a straight line marked on the floor at a 90-degree angle to the mirror to step on. You can use tape or chalk to mark the line or use a seam or crack already on the floor. The line is used to check if your movement is in a straight line. A countdown stopwatch or a timer with a buzzer will be helpful for these exercises.

A safety note: it is the responsibility of the advancing partner to take care not to move the retreating partner into a dangerous situation, such as hitting a wall or tripping over something.

### *1A. Advances*

These first drills will assist you in learning the advance and retreat while maintaining a proper on guard position. Start on guard facing the mirror, about 6 to 10 meters (19.8 to 32.8 feet) away, with the line on the floor intersecting the middle of the front foot and your rear heel just touching the line. Place your hands on your hips. Hold body erect during the exercise. Feet must be placed correctly on the line for each step.

*Success Goal =* Complete 10 advances toward the mirror in perfect form with feet correctly placed on line____

### Success Check
• Position knees over your shoelaces____
• Keep shoulders and hips level and in line____
• Hold chin up____
• Keep center of gravity between your feet____

### To Increase Difficulty
• Place arms in on guard position.
• Close your eyes and make the advances; check the position of your feet after completing the footwork.
• Make advances as quickly as possible while maintaining good form.

### To Decrease Difficulty
• Advance slowly using smaller steps.
• Pause after each advance and check your body position and placement of your feet on line.

### 1B. Flight Drill—Retreats

On guard with your hands on your hips, close to and facing the mirror with feet correctly placed on the line. Retreat 10 times. Remember that your front foot, which finishes the retreat, needs to feel like it moves faster and a shorter distance than the rear foot, which starts the retreat.

**Success Goal =** Complete 10 retreats keeping feet on the line. Repeat this set 5 times____

**Success Check**
• Move rear foot first___
• Do not allow body to tilt forward to lift rear foot___
• Keep knees bent over your shoelaces___

**To Increase Difficulty**
• Place arms in on guard position.
• Bend knees more.
• Make retreats faster.
• Do not look at the line until you finish the retreats.
• Close your eyes and retreat 10 times, then open your eyes and check your position on the line.

**To Decrease Difficulty**
• Pause and check position after each retreat.

## 1C. Advances or Retreats

On guard in the center of the floor. Close your eyes. Your partner moves from where you last saw her. She stops somewhere on the floor and calls your name once. You must advance to or retreat from her without opening your eyes, and stop in front of her. Your partner must remain in the place from which she called you. She evaluates your advances or retreats and distance perception.

**Success Goal** = Perform correct advances or retreats in a straight line to exactly the spot where you think she is and stop in front of her___

### ✔ Success Check

• Relax shoulders and stay in proper on guard position___
• Focus on the location of the sound___
• Advance aggressively using small steps___
• Press rear hip down___

### To Increase Difficulty

• Turn around once after your partner calls your name and then advance to or retreat from her.

### To Decrease Difficulty

• Have partner come closer to you and call.

## 2A. Mobility With Partner

This second set of drills will assist you in learning to use the advance and retreat to maintain distance between you and your partner. Start on guard facing your partner with a distance of one meter (approximately three feet) between your extended arms. Your front arm should be three-quarters extended. During the drill, your partner is the leader; he makes two advances, you retreat two times, he retreats three times, and you advance three times. Maintain the same distance between you and your partner throughout the drill. It is your responsibility to keep the distance constant because you are following. This is called "keeping distance."

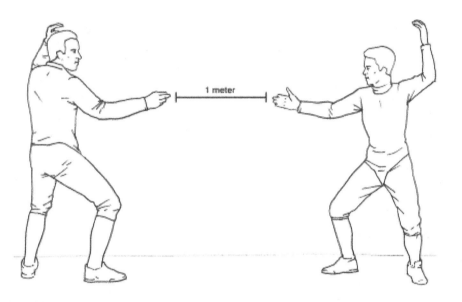

1 meter

**Success Goal =** Keep distance with your partner for 30 seconds, continuing to repeat the advance and retreat sequence, resting 30 seconds in between. Repeat this set five times___

**Success Check**
• Check your distance constantly___
• Have partner check your on guard position___
• Keep your eyes on your opponent's shoulder area or face___
• Keep your elbow pointed toward the floor, with your forearm parallel to the floor for epee or slightly angled up for foil___

**To Increase Difficulty**
• Partner changes tempo or rhythm of steps.
• Partner makes subtle fakes with the body.
• Increase work time to one minute. Increase number of sets. If fatigue attacks, you may increase rest time to one minute.
• Keep feet correctly placed on line.

**To Decrease Difficulty**
• Change the footwork pattern, decreasing advances and retreats by one.
• Place your hands on your hips.
• Leader pauses after each step.
• Decrease work time; increase rest time.

## 2B. Mobility, Changing Direction

For this drill you will need a rope about 1 1/2 meters (5 feet) long. Face your partner in an on guard position with your feet correctly placed on the line. You and your partner each hold the rope in your weapon hand. Position your hands on the rope with your arms three-quarters extended so that the rope sags slightly and there is a distance of about 1 meter (3 1/2 feet) between you and your partner's hands.

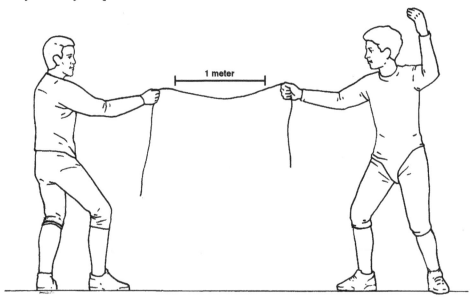

1 meter

Your partner makes three advances and two retreats or retreats three times and advances two times. You must respond with the appropriate footwork to maintain constant distance. Use the rope as a visual aid to alert you when you are not keeping the correct distance.

The leader should move slowly so the partner can keep correct distance and maintain good form. Keep your feet correctly placed on the line on the floor. Your weapon arm is slightly bent and does not move to adjust the amount of slack in the rope. The distance between you and your partner should be maintained by moving your feet at the appropriate time, the correct speed, and the correct distance dictated to you by your partner's movement. Do not allow your body to sway back and forth to keep distance.

Leader advances and retreats, partner follows, trying to maintain correct distance to keep the rope taut. Both fencers must maintain good form.

**Success Goal** = Your partner leads and you follow for 30 seconds and then rest 30 seconds. Then you lead and rest 30 seconds. Repeat five times___

**Success Check**
• Relax shoulders___
• Take small steps___
• Maintain good on guard position___
• Don't guess; move when your partner moves, not before___

**To Increase Difficulty**
• Leader changes the footwork pattern of three and two.
• Increase work time and number of sets.
• Change direction quickly and often.
• Bend knees more.

**To Decrease Difficulty**
• Change footwork to advancing 12 meters and retreating 12 meters
• Pause after each step.
• Pause after each change of direction.
• Reduce work time or number of sets.

## 2C. Mobility With Distance Control

On guard facing your partner, extend your weapon arm and touch your palms together but do not hold. Arms are extended. You lead and your partner must keep distance. You advance two times and then retreat three times or retreat two times and advance three times. Your partner keeps distance by responding with the appropriate footwork. Your hands can slide back and forth a little but must always be in contact. Stay in a good balanced on guard position and focus on keeping your knees bent during change of direction.

**Success Goal =** 30 seconds mobility with 30 seconds rest. Change leaders after each set. Repeat this set five times____

**Success Check**
• Relax shoulders___
• Change direction smoothly___
• Keep arms extended___
• Keep fingers extended___

**To Increase Difficulty**
• Leader varies from the predetermined footwork pattern.
• Leader changes rhythm of steps.
• Leader varies the length of the steps.
• Bend knees more.

**To Decrease Difficulty**
• Advance 12 meters and then retreat 12 meters.
• Leader pauses after change of direction.
• Leader makes small steps.
• Decrease work time; increase rest time.
• Slow the drill down.

### 3. Bouncing, Dynamic Mobility

This drill adds the bouncing element while maintaining the proper on guard position. Start on guard facing the mirror about 4 meters (12 feet) away. Bounce 10 times in place, then bounce two times forward, then advance two times and retreat three times. Repeat three times. This is one set. Focus on body position and balance when you change direction. Have your partner evaluate your progress after each set. Constantly check your position in the mirror.

**Success Goal** = Complete 10 sets. Rest 30 seconds after each set_____

### Success Check

- Bounce, using the feet. Do not use the knees to bounce___
- Make small bounces, stay light on your feet___
- Keep head level with limited bobbing___
- Change direction smoothly and quickly without pausing___

### To Increase Difficulty

- Increase number of in-place bounces to 20.
- Bend knees more.
- Move as quickly as possible, keeping correct form.
- Make change of direction quicker than bouncing tempo.

### To Decrease Difficulty

- Reduce number of bounces.
- Pause after each set.
- Slow the drill down.

### *4. Progressive Distance Drill With Partner*

The purpose of this drill is to teach you how to keep distance while you and your partner are performing different types of footwork. This drill is difficult even for Olympic team members, so go slowly and develop your skills. After you start bouting it is important not to be dominated by your opponent's rhythm. You must keep your own rhythm and try to dominate your opponent. You move with your opponent but are not controlled by him—a difficult concept but when you feel it, you will recognize it.

Purchase a wooden dowel about 1 cm in diameter and 1 meter (3-1/2 feet) long. Place a tennis ball on one end of the dowel for padding (stick the dowel halfway through the ball).

Get on guard facing your partner. Hold the dowel in your weapon hand. Place the end of the dowel with the tennis ball on your partner's chest, just below his collar bone with your arm extended three-quarters. Your partner is the leader. Maintain distance by moving your feet quickly at the appropriate time in response to your partner. You may flex and extend your weapon arm slightly but try to keep distance by moving your feet and not moving your arm or body. Your goal is to keep the tennis ball on the leader's chest during all of the following footwork variations. After you begin fencing, do this drill regularly to improve your conditioning, focus, distance perception, and feel for the bout. If you are short of time, be sure to do drill 5. After you have your equipment, do the drill with your weapon and be fully dressed for bouting.

**Success Goal =** Complete all drills with each of the footwork variations: 20 seconds work with 30 seconds rest___

Perform the following drills with footwork variations, always reaching to keep the ball on your partner's chest.

1. You and your partner move by stepping (advancing and retreating).
2. You and your partner bounce.
3. Partner bounces, you step.
4. Partner steps, you bounce.
4a. Your partner advances the length of the fencing strip or the space you have available. You retreat, keeping distance.
4b. Partner retreats the length of the fencing strip or the space you have available. You advance to keep the distance correct.
4c. Partner makes one advance and one retreat; you keep distance by using the appropriate footwork.
4d. Partner makes three advances and two retreats; you keep distance by using the appropriate footwork.
4e. Partner moves back and forth without a predetermined footwork pattern; you keep distance by using the appropriate footwork.

**Success Check**

### Advancing
- Keep front knee over laces___
- Keep knees bent and pressing out___
- Lift front toe first___
- Keep shoulders relaxed and arm fully extended (not locked)___

### Retreating
- Relax___
- Keep chin up___
- Keep rear hip level with front hip___
- Keep shoulders level___
- Don't shift weight to your front foot to lift your rear foot___

### Bouncing
- Relax shoulders___
- Feet leave floor at the same time
- Both feet land at the same time___
- Bounce using feet, not knees
- Keep heels slightly off the floor___

### To Increase Difficulty
- Partner varies the rhythm and size of the footwork.
- Partner does body fakes.
- Partner changes direction quickly.
- Increase work time or sets.

### To Decrease Difficulty
- Partner pauses after each step to allow partner time to adjust.
- Decrease work time; increase rest time.

## 5. FencAerobic—Footwork Training Program

Additional training to improve your footwork and conditioning; timing and distance will improve if you do the drills with a partner.

You may perform the following drills for time or by distance, or do the suggested number of sets.

a. Warm-up—Jump rope 1 minute, rest 1 minute, repeat 5 times. Rest 2 minutes, then jump rope continuously for 2 minutes.

b. 30 seconds, advancing (or 20 advances or 10 meters distance × 3)
30 seconds rest

c. 30 seconds, retreating, (or 20 retreats or 10 meters distance × 3)
30 seconds rest

d. 30 seconds, 4 advances, 2 retreats, 3 bounces (or repeat series 5 times)
30 seconds rest

e. 30 seconds, 3 retreats, 2 advances, 4 bounces (or repeat series 5 times)
30 seconds rest

f. 30 seconds, bounce in place (or 60 bounces). Bend your knees to the max.
30 seconds rest

g. 30 seconds, 1 bounce forward, 1 bounce backward (or × 30)
30 seconds rest

h. 30 seconds, 3 bounces forward, 1 bounce back (or × 20)
30 seconds rest

i. 30 seconds, 3 bounces backward, 1 bounce forward (or × 20)
30 seconds rest

j. 30 seconds, 2 bounces forward, 2 advances, 2 bounces backward (or × 10)
30 seconds rest

k. 30 seconds, 4 bounces backward, 2 bounces forward (or × 10)
30 seconds rest

l. 30 seconds. 3 advances, 2 bounces backward, 2 bounces forward, 3 retreats (or × 10)

**Success Goal** = Do the entire program without compromising form. Stay on a straight line___

### To Increase Intensity

• Flex your knees more.
• Make your steps faster and shorter, change direction aggressively and quickly without stopping.
• Do the entire workout in a very low on guard position.

### To Decrease Intensity

• Flex your knees less.
• Take steps slowly. Pause before changing direction.
• Shorten exercise time and increase rest periods.

The footwork can be done in a variety of ways:

1. Do it alone, for technique, for specific muscular conditioning or for speed.
2. Do it facing a mirror (excellent for analysis and for technique).
3. Do footwork with a partner/coach critiquing your performance, position, and technique.
4. With a partner for distance, timing, training, and awareness.
5. Change leadership roles each set, or you can lead the entire exercise and your partner can lead the following day.

## Success Stoppers

A large stumbling block to many fencers is setting an unobtainable goal—such as "everything must be perfect today." Fencing is a long-term commitment. Improvements must be made every day. Know your purpose and set your goals before each fencing activity; decide what you want your outcome to be. Don't be realistic—that's an excuse for being negative. Be a dreamer. Don't try to be perfect, just be better than yesterday. Just 1 percent better. Keep a detailed journal of your training. Focus on what you do right.

### SUCCESS SUMMARY

Build your fencing game around a balanced on guard position and quick footwork advances, retreats, and bounces. The fencer who can move quickly on the strip in a balanced position can attack and defend when the time is right. Just remember balance is the key. Start in the on guard position and remember that each advance, retreat, or bounce should place you in a position ready for any surprise. Movements forward or backward by advance, retreat, or bounce are small, the knees remain bent, and the feet are kept close to the floor during each movement.

We have explored the basic on guard position and mobility. The major element in fencing is the zone between two fencers. Footwork is necessary to command this space. Territorial control or distance management is basic for you to be successful in your fencing endeavor.

You now have completed the preliminary stages of footwork necessary in learning how to fence. After you have successfully completed all of the drills you will begin to feel comfortable in the fencing position and embark upon the concept of space management without sacrificing your form.

# HITTING THE TARGET: DETERMINING APPROPRIATE DISTANCE

The second step in becoming a fencer is selecting your handle and your weapon. Before you become concerned with the other intricacies of fencing you must become comfortable with your weapon. You must learn how to hold it, how far it extends your reach, and how to control your point. Learning to control the point of your weapon and knowing your distance are essential to the sport of fencing.

## Why Is Accurate Point Control Important?

In Step 1 you learned how to use your legs to move on the strip, giving you the ability to move into the right distance to score a hit. In this step you will learn to deliver the hit accurately. All touches are made up of three elements: proper footwork, accurate handwork, and good mental choices and tactics in selecting the appropriate course of action. All are necessary for you to score on your opponent. Getting accustomed to the weapon and the correct distance is of prime importance to you because the purpose of fencing is to hit the opponent accurately and in a timely manner, with the point of the weapon from the correct distance before your opponent can score on you. Throughout this book we will continually ask you to determine your correct distance.

## Selecting a Grip

The selection of the appropriate grip for your hand is the starting point for hitting accurately. Two of the most popular types of handles are the French

grip and the pistol grip. The French grip is a straight type and is recommended for beginners. The French handle helps the beginner to learn to manipulate the point with the fingers as well as develop strength in the hand (diagram 2.1).

The pistol grips are a group of handles that are shaped to fit the hand and allow you a firm grip with control. Each type of pistol grip has a slightly different configuration, but all are designed to give each finger a specific position.

There are advantages and disadvantages to both the French grip and the pistol grip. The pistol grip allows for better blade control during the course of fencing. Perhaps this is why at least 90 percent of foil fencers and about 70 percent of epee fencers use the pistol grip. Some epee fencers use the French grip for the additional length and may alternate between the two handles, depending on the opponent.

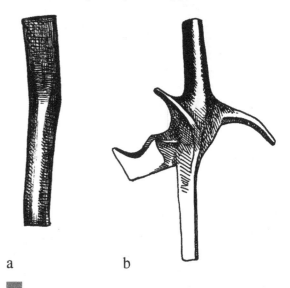

a                    b

**Diagram 2.1**     French grip (a) and pistol grip (b).

Hold the handle as you would a bird—not too tightly, not too loosely. With whichever grip you decide upon, you now must learn the proper finger position to maintain control of your point and the correct amount of force to hold the handle. It is very hard to change to French from pistol, so start with the French and then change to pistol later if you like. It is similar to learning to drive a manual shift car and then changing to automatic.

### Holding the French Grip— Basic Position

The thumb and forefinger pinch the handle just behind, but not touching, the guard, as shown in figure 2.1. The remaining three fingers wrap around the handle. Place your thumb on the wide, flat side of the handle. The curve of the handle should be toward your palm. The end of the handle, the pommel, should be in contact with your wrist. The weapon and your forearm should form a straight line.

The manipulation of the point by the fingers to make the precise movements required in fencing should be done with the same control and pressure you use to write or draw. The position of the hand is slightly rotated out, which places the thumb at about 1 o'clock for right-handed fencers and about 11 o'clock for left-handed fencers.

There are two alternate positions for holding the French handle in order to gain extra distance. Start with the same hand position as above. Then slip your hand backward on the handle until you are holding the last 8 to 10 centimeters (3-1/4 to 4 inches) of the handle. In this position you gain several inches of reach but lose some power and control. You also can hold the French grip with the forefinger fully extended along the side of the handle. This helps to give some people a little better control of the point, while still gaining extra distance.

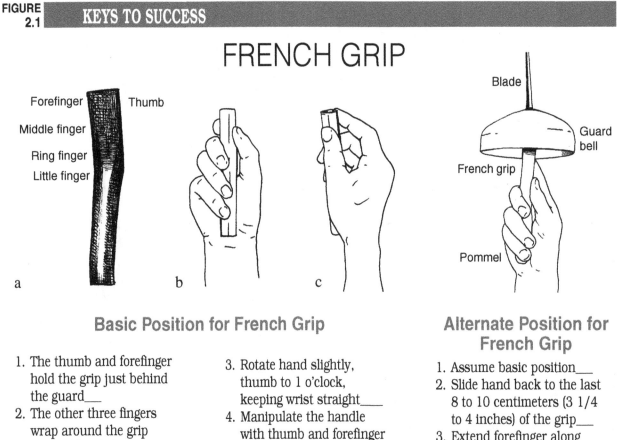

**FIGURE 2.1** KEYS TO SUCCESS

# FRENCH GRIP

**Basic Position for French Grip**

1. The thumb and forefinger hold the grip just behind the guard___
2. The other three fingers wrap around the grip holding firmly but not too tightly___
3. Rotate hand slightly, thumb to 1 o'clock, keeping wrist straight___
4. Manipulate the handle with thumb and forefinger and anchor with little finger___

**Alternate Position for French Grip**

1. Assume basic position___
2. Slide hand back to the last 8 to 10 centimeters (3 1/4 to 4 inches) of the grip___
3. Extend forefinger along the side of the grip for better control___

### Holding a Pistol Grip

The pistol grip has a specific groove for each finger. The thumb is on the top side of the grip, slightly bent, and pointing toward the tip of the blade. Pinch the handle between the thumb and first digit of your forefinger. The remainder of the fingers fall into place as in figure 2.2.

Hold and manipulate the pistol grip firmly with the forefinger, thumb, and the little finger. The two middle fingers are used to help maintain control of the weapon. Do not hold too tightly with the middle two fingers because it locks your fingers and wrist.

**FIGURE 2.2** | **KEYS TO SUCCESS**

# PISTOL GRIP

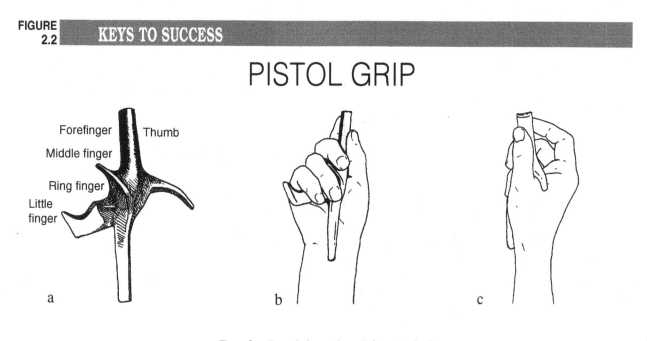

Forefinger Thumb
Middle finger
Ring finger
Little finger

a    b    c

**Basic Position for Pistol Grip**

1. Thumb on top of grip___
2. Forefinger is bent on bottom of grip ___

3. Squeeze the grip between the thumb and forefinger___
4. Position the other 3 fingers in their places on the pistol grip___

## Preparing a Practice Target

In this step we will use practice targets, a mirror, and your training partner. The practice target will permit you to hit it again and again until you can feel the appropriate distance to hit firmly. You must hit hard enough to depress the tip 750 grams (26.5 ounces) in epee and 500 grams (17.6 ounces) in foil. The mirror allows you to see so that your action is executed correctly. Hitting your training partner assists you in learning how to hit the real target area, which is neither static nor in a flat plane.

Before you start the drills in this step, you'll need to prepare a target. The target should be a rectangle approximately 20 by 30 centimeters (8 by 12 inches). The target can be a piece of wood, padded and covered with rubber, leather, or other durable soft material. Attach the target firmly to a wall with the center approximately 120 to 140 centimeters (47 to 55 inches) from the floor, depending on your height. To position the target, get on guard with your weapon and extend your arm the same level as your shoulder. The center of the target should be at this level.

## *Extension*

Direct your point to the target and follow this immediately by extending your arm, lifting, and straightening your elbow. Do not lock your elbow. Touch the target at shoulder height with the tip of your weapon. For foil the bell should be the same level as the tip. For epee the bell should be slightly higher than the point at which it contacts the target. Do not move your torso. Concentrate on one thing, the weapon, and how it is part of your body, a mere extension of your arm. You should press the tip of your weapon toward the target rather than poke or punch at it. After you hit the target hold your position for a moment and then recover to the on guard position. Do it slowly and precisely. It is important to achieve proper technique and visually memorize the distance from which you can hit from the on guard position.

# How to Touch the Target

Position yourself in front of the target in an on guard position. Be sure your rear arm is in a relaxed position so as not to cause tension in your shoulders (figure 2.3a shows on guard for foil; 2.3c shows position for epee). Extend your arm while holding your weapon. Be sure your shoulders and neck are relaxed. Move toward or away from the target, adjusting both feet until the distance is such that the point of your weapon touches the target with enough force to slightly bend the blade upward (figure 2.3b shows the extension with foil;

2.3d shows epee). This is your *extension distance*. The distance between a fencer and her opponent, which requires solely the extension of the arm to hit the designated target area, is referred to as extension distance. Do not lean forward and push on your weapon. Keep the body erect and relaxed. This is strictly an arm exercise.

After the hit, return to the on guard position. This means relaxing your weapon arm and bending at the elbow slightly (foil one-third extended, epee two-thirds extended). The forearm and weapon should be parallel to the floor for epee and slightly up from parallel for foil. The weapon and forearm should form one straight line from the elbow to the tip of your weapon. Keep your head up and your shoulders down and back.

## *Focus on the Target*

Concentration and precise execution are the keys to benefiting from your drills and to aiding your future growth in fencing. Taking your mind off the target is worse than taking your eyes off the target. Start with short test periods and extend them as your concentration improves. For five extensions, focus completely on the task, then increase the number of extensions as your focus improves.

Before you do the drills in this book, close your eyes and visualize the action as you want it to be. Feel it, see it, and allow your body to reproduce this image. Visualize each action before you perform it.

**FIGURE
2.3**   KEYS TO SUCCESS

# TOUCHING THE TARGET

a

b

## Preparation

1. On guard extension distance from target__

2. Keep your weapon point, elbow, shoulder, hip, knee, and front foot in the same vertical plane with point directed to the target __

c

d

## Execution

1. Move point toward the target__
2. Keep chin slightly up with eyes on the target__
3. Extend your arm, pressing point to the target; blade should bend slightly up__

4. On contact the bell should be slightly higher than the point for epee and the same level as the point for foil

## Recovery

1. Return to on guard position as in figure a and b__
2. Keep point directed toward the target__

## SUCCESS STOPPERS

A correct touch requires proper *technique* executed at the right time from the appropriate *distance*.

| Error | Correction |
|---|---|
| 1. Hitting too hard. | 1. Do not punch the target or use your torso to hit. |
| 2. Missing the target. | 2. Start point first and press point forward. Keep eyes on target. Do not blink. |
| 3. Tensing and raising your shoulders. | 3. Keep your shoulders relaxed and down. |
| 4. Bending your wrist. | 4. Keep wrist straight; your forearm and blade must be in one line. |

It is important that the handwork be as accurate as the footwork is mobile. You must be able to feel the hit. Use the practice target, the mirror, and your training partner to perfect the movement and the feel of your touch. In this step we focus on isolating the hand action, with limited foot movement, to build the muscle memory necessary to instinctively move the hand forward to make a hit.

## HITTING THE TARGET DRILLS

The purpose of these drills is to help you "feel and control your point"—to become familiar with your arm position, your weapon, and distance, and how to extend your arm without tension in your shoulder.

Get on guard, in extension distance away from the target. Do not lean to get the correct distance. Hit the target with the point of the weapon. Your weapon should bend slightly up as you hit. Keep your wrist, elbow, shoulder, hip, knee, and front foot in the same vertical plane.

You and your training partner must be in full fencing uniform during all pair drills. Both fencers must salute and put their masks on before approaching each other for the fencing drills.

### *1. Mirror Image*

Assume a good on guard position with your weapon aimed toward the mirror. The foil tip should be higher than the bell guard. The epee tip should be level with the top of your bell guard. For both foil and epee, be sure that a straight line is formed from the tip of the weapon to your elbow.

Extend your arm toward the mirror, positioning your arm and weapon so you do not see the reflection of your forearm in the mirrror. It should be hidden by the bell guard. Memorize this position. Close your eyes, lower the point of your weapon to touch the floor, and return to on guard, open your eyes, and check your position. Be sure you are far enough away from the mirror so that you do not hit it when you extend your arm. Be careful—the image in the mirror is deceptive, and you can reach farther than you think.

Practice closing your eyes and dropping and raising your blade, with forearm and weapon remaining in a straight line.

**Success Goal =** 10 consecutive correct positions___

**Success Check**
* Forearm hidden behind bell guard ___
* Return arm to good on guard position ___
* Shoulder down, head up___
* Stabilize elbow___
* Keep wrist straight___
* Keep body still___

**To Increase Difficulty**
* Close your eyes and move your hand and arm around in a circle and then return to on guard position. Open your eyes and check your position.
* Place your weapon on the floor instead of pointing at the floor. Pick it up and return to on guard position.

**To Decrease Difficulty**
* Have your partner stand in front of you and critique you, instead of using a mirror (be careful not to hit your partner). Your partner needs to stand 3 to 4 meters (10 to 13 feet) in front of you. He tells you when your position is correct or what to do to correct it.

## 2. Extension to the Target

The purpose of this drill is to create precision in your thrust. This drill should not be rushed. You need to concentrate on your technique and feel the fluidity of your motion, culminating with the hit on the target.

From on guard position at extension distance from the target, extend 10 times, hitting the center of the target (figures a and b). Extend smoothly at about the speed you would use to pick up a pencil—neither quickly nor slowly.

a

b

**Success Goal** = 10 consecutive hits in center target ___

### Success Check
- Relax your shoulders___
- Press your point to the target___
- Accelerate to the target___
- Move only your arm; do not allow any other part of your body to move or shift to hit the target___

### To Increase Difficulty
- Sit lower in the on guard position.
- Extend quickly and smoothly.
- Do not pause between hits. Make actions continuously, but not rapid fire.

### To Decrease Difficulty
- Extend slowly.
- Set a goal of two consecutive hits, then increase the goal by two until you reach 10.

### 3. Vertical Plane Hits

Get on guard at extension distance from the target. Bend your arm and point the weapon at the ceiling, then lower the weapon until it points at the target. Extend, hit the target. Next, from the on guard position, without moving the elbow, lower the forearm until the blade is pointing diagonally toward the floor. Then raise the forearm until the weapon is pointing at the target. Extend and hit the center of the target.

**Success Goal =** 10 hits on the center of the target from each of the positions___

**Success Check**
• Keep wrist straight and firm with weapon and forearm forming one straight line ___
• Slowly press the point forward with precision___
• Don't move your elbow around___

### To Increase Difficulty
• Extend quickly, accelerating to the target.
• Close your eyes.
• Remain in on guard position between hits; do not straighten legs and relax.
• Hit the target in a different designated area.

### To Decrease Difficulty
• Extend slowly.
• After hit, keep point on the target a minimum of two seconds.

## 4. Horizontal Plane Hits

Put numbers in the corners of your target—from upper left, working clockwise: 4, 6, 8, 7. (See figure below.) Get on guard facing target. Keep the forearm and weapon as one straight line and your elbow down and slightly in toward your body. Begin your extension to the center of the target; during your extension direct the point of the weapon to the upper left corner of the target where you hit. Return to on guard position. Repeat procedure to each of the other corners.

This drill may be done with a partner. Get on guard facing one another at your extension distance. Mark numbers on your partner's jacket with chalk. Extend and hit each number in a clockwise progression.

a

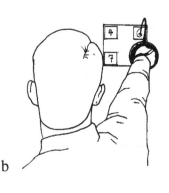

b

**Success Goal** = 10 hits to each corner of the target___

### Success Check

• Keep wrist straight and firm___
• Press the point forward with precision___
• Maneuver point with your fingers___

### To Increase Difficulty

• Extend quickly, accelerating to the target.
• Call the number you are to hit after you begin the extension.
• Repeat with an advance from advance distance.
• Have your partner call the number you are to hit after you begin your extension.

### To Decrease Difficulty

• Extend slowly.
• Call the number before you extend.
• Point to the corner you choose to hit before you begin the extension.

## 5. Quick Hits

The purpose of this drill is to help you learn to thrust and relax your arm quickly, keeping your arm soft and not rigid, essential in foil and very important in epee. In this drill you must hit the center of the target two times in quick succession. Both hits should take place within one-half second, close to the time it takes to knock twice quickly on a door. In this drill your arm does not return to the on guard position between the two hits. Merely relax your arm, allowing the point to come off the target a couple of inches, then fully extend again, smoothly.

**Success Goal** = 10 double hits in the center of the target. ___

**Success Check**
• Keep shoulders relaxed___
• Keep extension smooth, do not punch ___
• Keep body steady and balanced___
• Raise bell slightly with hit for epee ___

**To Increase Difficulty**
• Extend arm and advance to target.
• Do the drill with a partner.
• Partner calls for a single hit or double hit.
• Call your choice of single or double hit after you begin your extension.
• Add a third and fourth hit, changing the tempo.

**To Decrease Difficulty**
• Make hits slower.
• Stop after each hit.

## 6. Spiral Hits

Get in the on guard position. Make five circles clockwise with the tip of your blade as your point spirals toward the target. Use your fingers to make the circles as small as possible. Limit your wrist movement. Hit center target with full extension. Do the same while making a counterclockwise spiral.

**Success Goal** = 10 consecutive hits from clockwise spiral and from counterclockwise spiral on the center of the target___

**Success Check**
• Relax shoulders___
• Make blade movements smooth and continuous___
• For epee, raise bell guard slightly as you hit the target. For foil keep the bell guard level with point___

**To Increase Difficulty**
• Perform spirals with an advance.
• Spiral two times clockwise and two times counterclockwise before touching target.
• Make the circles smaller and faster, finish with full extension to target.

**To Decrease Difficulty**
• Reduce the spirals to two before hitting the target.
• Make circles without extending your arm. After you have completed the requisite number of circles, extend your arm and touch the target.

### 7. Moving Target I

Since your opponent will rarely be standing still, it is important to be able to hit a moving target. This drill trains not only your hand but your eyes. You must time your hit so that the target is at the proper distance and directly in front of you at the time your extension is completed.

Attach a string to a golf ball or tennis ball and hang it from the ceiling. The ball should be at the height of your extension when you are in the on guard position.

Get on guard at your extension distance to the ball. Swing the ball gently from side to side. Extend your arm and repeatedly tap the ball gently with the point of the weapon without moving your legs or shifting your weight.

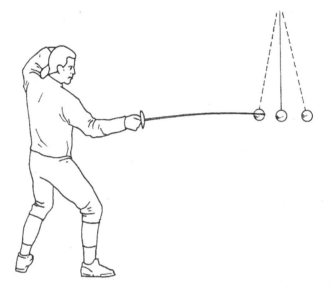

**Success Goal =**
- Hit ball 5 times in succession ____
- Count the number of hits you can make in one minute____

**Success Check**
- Relax shoulders____
- Keep body in good on guard position____
- Hit ball gently and keep point close to the ball____
- Keep your eyes on the ball____
- Do not use your body to hit the ball; keep your body quiet and simply extend your arm____
- Extend smoothly; don't punch the ball____

**To Increase Difficulty**
- Advance to hit the ball. Be sure to move point first.
- Use a smaller ball.
- Increase number of consecutive hits

**To Decrease Difficulty**
- Use a larger ball.
- Don't swing ball.
- Stop ball after each hit.

## 8. Moving Target II

Get on guard at extension distance to a stationary target. Have your training partner hold a glove 15 to 20 centimeters (6 to 8 inches) above the center of the target (figure a). When your partner drops the glove, try to pin the glove to the target by thrusting to the target as the glove drops. Draw lines or a colored area for points as in figure b. The higher on the chart you catch the glove, the quicker you are and the more points you earn. You must relax and focus on the glove with your peripheral vision.

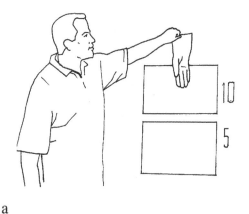

a

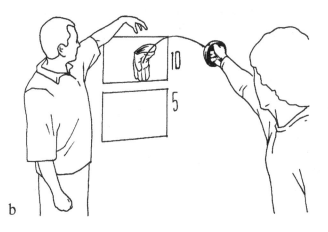

b

**Success Goal** = 5 pins out of 10 drops____

### Success Check
- Relax and keep body calm____
- Focus on moving point first____
- Raise bell slightly higher than point at moment of hit for epee____
- Do not look directly at glove; use your peripheral vision____

### To Increase Difficulty
- Partner holds glove lower.
- Partner fakes before dropping the glove.
- Partner talks to you about anything, just to distract you.
- On guard advance distance away from target. Partner holds glove higher, and you pin glove, but you must make an advance to reach target.

### To Decrease Difficulty
- Partner holds glove higher above target.
- Partner gives signal before dropping glove.

## HITTING THE TARGET SUCCESS SUMMARY

You have been practicing to control the point of your weapon and extend your arm correctly. These elements are critical to successful fencing. The sooner you perfect a smooth, quick, relaxed arm extension, the more success you will have in hitting the target. The sport of fencing awards points only for hitting the target; there are no style points. Accurate point control is an important key to hitting your opponents. The practice drills in this step provide a variety of ways to improve your accuracy and consistency. Try to improve 1 percent every day. Soon you will be able to hit the target with speed and accuracy.

Go back to Step 1 and do the footwork drills with your weapon and a partner.

# STEP

## 3

# THRUST, LUNGE, AND RECOVERY: DELIVERING THE HIT TO YOUR OPPONENT

At the World Fencing Championships you will see many very complicated actions involving a variety of footwork and handwork. But in an overwhelming majority of the hits, the thrust is the basic blade movement used to begin the action, and the lunge is the footwork used to deliver the hit to the opponent. The recovery from the lunge is critical, so you will not be scored on if your initial attack is not successful. The straight thrust can be an attack by itself, or it can be the first step of a more complex attack, beginning with the thrust used as a feint. There is virtually an unlimited number of combinations and levels of difficulty of actions that can be built from the basic maneuvers, but remember, your hits are not weighted by style points or degree of difficulty. You score by hitting the opponent first and in foil, you may also receive the touch even though your opponent hits you first if you have priority. You gain priority if you start your attack first or beat the blade last. Over all, you are most successful if you use the simplest move the situation permits. The straight thrust is the foundation of most foil and epee touches.

When you deliver the thrust with a lunge, remember that once you begin a lunge, complete it; make the hit. Do not try to second-guess yourself and correct the lunge in the middle of the action. You need to recognize the areas in which you need to improve by asking after each hit: Did I hit (miss) because of my timing, distance, or technique? If technique was the factor, was it my blade work, footwork, or both? If tactics were the issue, was it my choice of action, was it the distance from which I did the action, or was it my timing? Did I miss because it was the wrong moment, or did I hit because it was the right moment? This quick analysis is beneficial and can be used throughout your life to continue to improve your fencing skills.

## Why Are Lunge and Recovery Important?

The purpose of learning the lunge and recovery is to empower you. These skills permit you to attack your opponent aggressively and make the hit. While the advance, retreat, and bounce give you the mobility necessary to get you within the appropriate distance to hit your opponent, a quick, decisive delivery mechanism is needed. The most commonly used device is the lunge. It can carry you a long distance with great speed. It will leave you, however, in an immobile position, from which it is difficult to defend. The recovery is the necessary complement to the lunge to avoid being hit after your attack in case you did not hit. It will take you back rapidly to the on guard position where the mobility you learned in Step 1 either can take you out of danger or bring you back into distance to attempt to deliver another hit.

# How to Execute a Straight Thrust (Straight Attack)

The straight attack is the same for foil and epee and is the simplest, fastest, and most effective attack. The hit is made by relaxing the shoulder and pressing and thrusting the point of weapon to the target (figures 3.1a and b).

The straight thrust may be either the initial action or the response to the action of the opponent. It is made by extending the sword arm with the point aimed toward any valid target area and may be accompanied with a variety of footwork, determined by how far away your opponent is, and in what direction he is moving at the time of your attack, forward or backward. The straight thrust is delivered by any of the footwork shown in Step 1 or with long footwork: the lunge or the fleche (demonstrated in step 9). You may score touches in foil on the opponent's torso or in epee anywhere on the opponent's body.

| FIGURE 3.1 | KEYS TO SUCCESS: STRAIGHT THRUST (STRAIGHT ATTACK) |
| --- | --- |

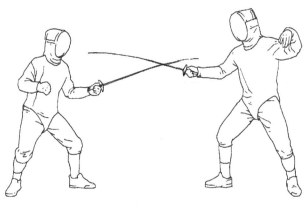

a

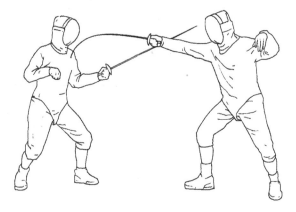

b

## Preparation

1. Get on guard with your lead foot pointing toward your opponent at extension or lunge distance. Extension distance is the distance at which you can hit the opponent simply by extending your arm. Lunge distance is the distance at which you can hit your opponent with a lunge ___

## Execution

1. Relax your shoulders___
2. Keep your eyes on intended target___
3. Thrust—extend arm fully___
4. Hit opponent firmly on the intended target___

## Follow-Up

1. Return to on guard position with eyes still on target___
2. Arm should recover to three-quarters extension___

The crucial element at this stage is relaxed technique. Be in correct balanced position before, during, and after the hit. Analyze what you did correctly; make improvements on your errors. Select only one fault to improve after each hit. Extend decisively, without punching.

| Error | Correction |
|---|---|
| 1. Tensing and raising your shoulder. | 1. Press shoulders down. |
| 2. Leaning back or forward with trunk during extension. | 2. Keep trunk slightly forward and still. Extend arm, keeping trunk stationary. |
| 3. Dropping bell guard; thrusting with a floppy wrist; your weapon and arm do not make a straight line. | 3. Hold weapon firmly with thumb, forefinger, and little finger. Press bell guard slightly up when point contacts target. Keep wrist firm and straight. Tighten the second and third fingers on the handle just a little. With French handle, keep pommel on the wrist. |

## Lunge

The lunge covers a longer distance than the advance. The lunge is a maneuver made with the legs as a means of delivering the hit. There are many different actions you can make with the blade before, during, and after the lunge.

### *Recovery From the Lunge*

The recovery, or the follow-up phase, in fencing is extremely important. This phase prepares you for the next action. You need to recover backward or forward immediately into an on guard position and be prepared for the next action.

### *When to Use the Lunge*

The lunge is used when the distance is such that you cannot reach your opponent with the point of your weapon by taking a single advance, but you could likely reach your opponent with two advances. A good moment for the straight attack is when the opponent picks up his front foot to move forward. Lunge when your opponent is moving forward with his front foot off the floor and is within your lunge distance. The lunge appears much faster when your opponent is moving toward you as opposed to moving away from you. The lunge

is traveling at the same speed, but the speed at which the hit occurs is much faster. If you attack an opponent who is standing still or is retreating, the time the opponent has to respond to your attack is much longer than the time the opponent has to respond if both of you are moving toward each other. This logic is the same as the speed at which two cars would hit if they were speeding toward one another versus if they were going in the same direction, or if the car being hit were standing still.

## How to Lunge

To execute the lunge you must first assume the on guard position (figure 3.2a). The lunge is just a long step with the front foot, without bringing the rear foot along. Lift your toes and step forward off the heel of the front foot, extending your front knee. Push with the rear leg while the front foot is in the air (figure 3.2b). The rear leg is the power for the lunge. The rear foot can slide forward but try to keep it three-quarters flat, allowing only the little toe side of the foot to come off the floor slightly. Do not allow the ankle of the rear foot to relax and collapse toward the floor. Maintain pressure on the floor with the ball of the foot and arch of the rear foot. If you force your foot to stick to the floor and do not allow it to slide, your lunge can never be longer than your legs, a severe disadvantage. The rear leg should be fully extended, briefly, as the front foot lands gently on the heel (figure 3.2c). The heel of the front foot strikes the floor first and rolls forward immediately onto the sole, finishing with the knee over the laces (figure 3.2d). Upon completion of the lunge the body is leaning slightly forward with the chin up and the back straight. Your shoulders and hips are parallel to the floor. The body remains in a state of controlled relaxation. A tense body does not react quickly.

If you are lunging for the first time, do not lunge more than one-half to three-quarters of the distance of which you are physically capable. Stretching before practicing the lunge is critical. The easiest muscle group to tear in fencing is located on the inside and back of the thigh. Those muscles are very vulnerable because they are stretched to the maximum during the lunge.

A short lunge done with the correct technique is far more effective than a long lunge done incorrectly. An incorrect and off-balance lunge puts you at a disadvantage, and you can easily fall prey to your opponent's hit.

During the lunge, it is important that the rear arm not interfere with the body's balance. The rear arm should extend over the rear leg as you lunge. It should remain in line with the shoulders and hips so as not to cause the body to twist or have to compensate for its incorrect placement or movement. The thumb should be up toward the ceiling with fingers open and relaxed.

The classic participation of the weapon arm in the lunge action is as follows: The point starts first to move forward as the arm begins to extend to the target. The extension of the arm finishes as the point hits the target just before the front foot lands. The lunge begins after the commencement of the extension but before the arm is fully extended. The completion of the extension gives impetus to the completion of the lunge. The front foot does not land until the point of the weapon has reached its destination. This is not easy to do. There are a variety of combinations of arm extension and timing for the lunge, but the one explained here is basic and essential. Master this one first, and the others can be incorporated into your game as your fencing personality develops and your strengths and weaknesses emerge. In foil the important thing is to be sure you have the right of way. You gain right of way by starting the attack first or beating the blade last. In epee the important thing is to be able to hit your opponent first, at least 1/25 of a second before she hits you.

**FIGURE 3.2** **KEYS TO SUCCESS: LUNGE**

### Preparation

1. On guard___
2. Extend weapon arm at shoulder level___
3. Leave arm extended___

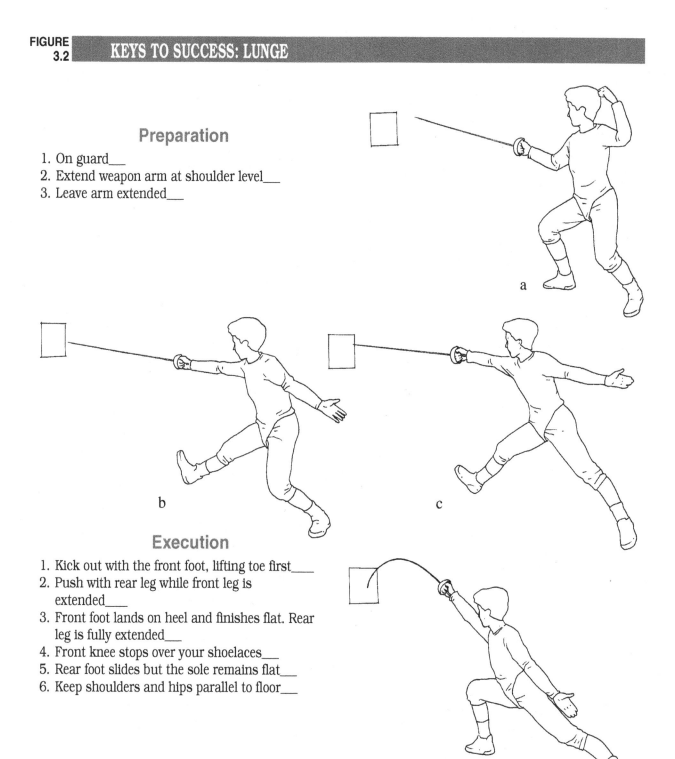

### Execution

1. Kick out with the front foot, lifting toe first___
2. Push with rear leg while front leg is extended___
3. Front foot lands on heel and finishes flat. Rear leg is fully extended___
4. Front knee stops over your shoelaces___
5. Rear foot slides but the sole remains flat___
6. Keep shoulders and hips parallel to floor___

### Follow-Up

1. Leave weapon arm softly extended briefly until legs are back in on guard position___
2. Recover forward or backward (illustrated in figures 3.3 and 3.4) to on guard position___

## LUNGE SUCCESS STOPPERS

Mistakes in the lunge cut across all levels of fencers. Even some world-class fencers don't get the full benefit from their lunge because of incorrect mechanics: front foot rising too high, head behind center of gravity, or body collapsing forward preventing a quick recovery. One mental stopper in performing a successful lunge is trying to lunge too far—losing sight of maintaining balance and keeping shoulders and hips level. The correct mechanics are not difficult; just practice the basics daily and do not sacrifice everything just to try to score a point. Strive for balance, control, and accuracy; this makes for consistent success throughout your fencing career.

| Errors | Corrections |
| --- | --- |
| 1. Lifting knee to lunge, lunging off toe. | 1. Raise toes slightly up, kick front foot forward, and lunge off your heel; extend front leg fully, reaching forward. |
| 2. Shifting weight back onto the rear foot to pick up front foot. | 2. Compress body forward slightly over thigh. Be sure rear leg is flexed and rear hip is down. This is necessary for you to be able to push with your rear leg. Kick out with your front foot. Don't try to get excessive distance or power. These will come after technique is mastered. |
| 3. Body collapsing too far forward on completion of lunge. | 3. Keep your head upright looking at target before, during, and after the hit. Keep back straight, shoulders level, and rear hip pressing down. Keep chin pointed at target and parallel to the floor. |
| 4. Raising rear hip higher than front hip, before, during, or after the lunge. | 4. Lower center of gravity; press rear hip toward floor during lunge and recovery. |
| 5. Not pushing with the rear leg and bending your rear knee in the lunge. | 5. Extend rear leg. Press on the floor with the ball and arch of foot. Hold rear knee extended for a brief period. |

## How to Recover Forward From the Lunge

To recover forward from the lunge you simply bring the rear leg into an on guard position with the least amount of body movement possible (figure 3.3). Shoulders and hips remain level; pay close attention to the rear hip—don't allow it to rise higher than the front hip. Keep the front foot and leg in good on guard position and bring the rear leg into the on guard position. Position your rear foot the correct distance from the front foot to regain the proper on guard. Do not push back with the front leg; allow your body to rise up slightly as you assume the on guard position. Be sure not to rock (shifting your weight from foot to foot) during the recovery. The recovery from the lunge also involves the hands and arms. As you recover, the rear arm returns to the on guard position. The weapon arm relaxes back into the on guard position, elbow bent.

FIGURE
3.3

## KEYS TO SUCCESS: RECOVER FORWARD FROM THE LUNGE

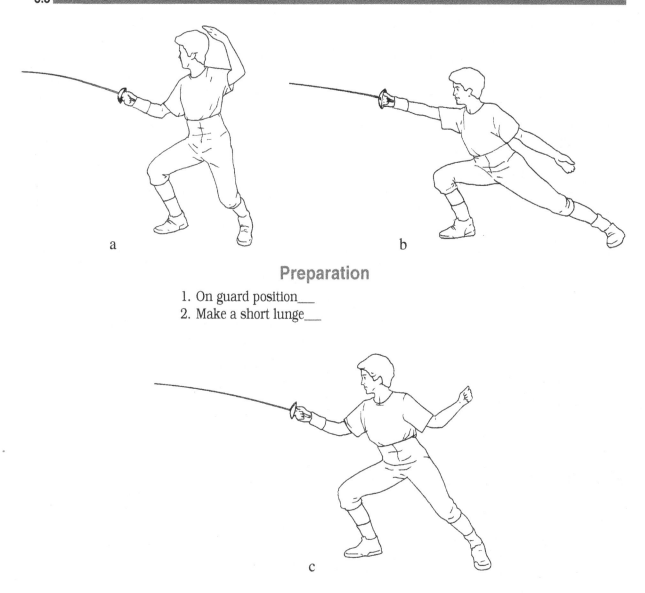

## Preparation

1. On guard position___
2. Make a short lunge___

## Execution Phase

1. Press body forward___
2. Snap rear leg forward into on guard at correct distance from front foot___
3. Return arms to on guard position___
4. Keep hips and shoulders level___

## Follow-Up

1. You are now in an on guard position___
2. Make two retreats or advances immediately___

The most common success stopper in recovering forward from the lunge is that many fencers consider the lunge as the end of the action and that also ends their concentration. The forward recovery from the lunge is as important as the lunge because you do not score with each lunge and many times it is what happens after the lunge that scores or causes you to be scored upon. It is the full attention to a very quick, balanced recovery that can advance you to the next level of fencing.

| Error | Correction |
|---|---|
| **Forward Recovery** | |
| 1. Pushing back with the front foot. | 1. Keep knees flexed and body pressing slightly forward. Front knee remains over laces. |
| 2. Straightening the legs. | 2. Keep front knee over the laces, as in the lunge and bring the rear leg forward. Keep body pressing forward. |
| 3. Closing feet together. | 3. Keep knees flexed in a deep on guard. Move rear foot quickly into the correct distance. |
| 4. Dropping head forward and raising rear hip to lift foot. | 4. Keep chest up and open. Don't take your eyes off your target. Keep chin up. |

## How to Recover Backward From the Lunge

To recover backward from the lunge, push off the front foot, bend the rear knee, keep your hips low and level, and return to the on guard position (figure 3.4). Snap your front foot backward, keeping your weight evenly distributed. Position your front foot, heel touching first, the correct distance from the rear foot to regain the proper on guard.

Keep your body pressing slightly forward. The rear hand recovers to the on guard position at the same time the front foot recovers. The weapon arm recovers to on guard position just after the front foot recovers.

**FIGURE 3.4**  **KEYS TO SUCCESS: RECOVER BACKWARD INTO AN ON GUARD POSITION**

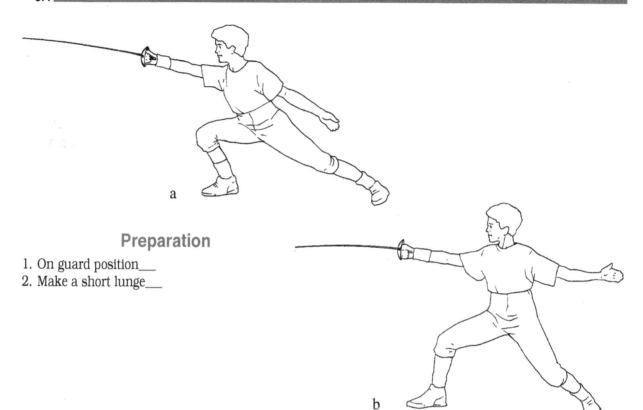

a

## Preparation

1. On guard position___
2. Make a short lunge___

b

## Execution

1. Push off front foot and bend rear knee, keeping hips level___
2. Bring front foot back, landing on the entire foot___
3. Place front foot the correct distance from the back foot___
4. Return arms to on guard___
5. Keep hips and shoulders level___
6. Keep head steady___

c

## Follow-Up

1. You are now in an on guard position___
2. Make two retreats or advances; be sure you are balanced___

## BACKWARD RECOVERY SUCCESS STOPPERS

The most common success stopper in recovering backward from the lunge is that many fencers consider the lunge as the end of the action and that also ends their concentration. The backward recovery from the lunge is as important as the lunge because you do not score with each lunge and many times it is what happens after the lunge that scores or causes you to be scored upon. It is the full attention to a very quick, balanced recovery that can advance you to the next level of fencing.

| Error | Correction |
|---|---|
| **Backward Recovery** | |
| 1. Dragging front heel. | 1. Pick up front foot, snap to on guard position. Chin up, back straight, and slightly arched. Make a shorter lunge. Strengthen your legs. |
| 2. Dropping weapon arm. | 2. Recover to the on guard position with weapon arm still extended toward target. Bend the weapon arm one second after completion of the recovery, keeping bell high. |
| 3. Keeping rear leg too straight. | 3. The rear leg bends immediately (think of sitting on a short stool on recovery) to the on guard position as the front foot pushes back. The rear knee may move in a semi-circle when recovering. Strengthen legs and hip area. |
| 4. Shifting weight back on to rear foot while recovering. | 4. Keep chin steady. Push off front foot; hips remain low to the ground. Bring front foot back quickly without rocking back onto the rear foot. Don't pull back with the shoulders and head. Head remains positioned over front hip. |

**THRUST, LUNGE, AND RECOVERY**

# DRILLS

The lunge is a powerful offensive tool, and forward and backward recoveries are both great defensive protection as well as preparation for the next offensive action. The lunge permits you to deliver a hit rapidly and from greater distance than the advance. The recovery enables you to be prepared for whatever may happen in the event that you do not score on the first action. Practice the movements slowly and carefully. Use a mirror to help you perfect and refine your technique. Your speed and power develop as your technique is perfected.

### 1. Lunge and Recover Back

On guard with your hands on your hips (figure a). Feet on a straight line facing a mirror or a partner. Take chalk and draw diagram of your feet on the floor in the on guard position. Make a short lunge and draw a diagram of where the front foot lands in the lunge (figure b). The purpose is to perfect the lunge movement; keep your hands on your hips so you can focus on the mechanics of your lunge.

**Success Goal =** 10 times lunge and backward recover to on guard with feet landing in the diagram you drew. ____

**Success Check: Lunge**
- Lift toes of front foot first ____
- Kick out with front foot____
- Rear leg pushes hard and finishes straight and locked____
- Land softly on your heel, roll on to flat of your foot ____
- Keep front knee over your shoelaces____

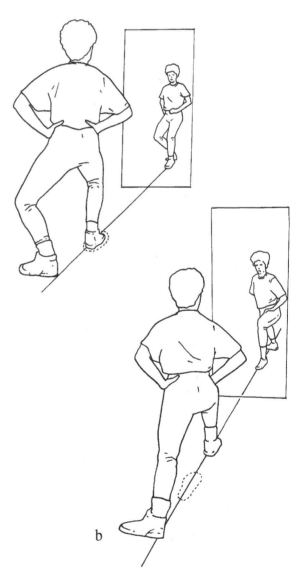

a

**Success Check: Recover Back**
- Bend rear knee____
- Push off front foot____
- Place front foot in on guard diagram____

b

### To Increase Difficulty

- Place bean bag or book on your head and lunges without dropping it.
- Complete 10 lunges without taking break.
- Place penny under your heel to be sure you are not lunging off your toe. You should kick penny several meters in front of you as you lunge.
- Draw three lines on the floor for the lunge: short, medium, and long. Do not increase the distance for medium and long very much.

### To Decrease Difficulty

- Make very small lunges.
- Check position after each lunge and recovery and take break after each recovery.

## 2. Lunge Accuracy

Hang a ball from the ceiling that measures about shoulder height when you are in your on guard position. This drill helps you to have a relaxed, controlled extension and not punch with your arm when you lunge. If you punch you will not hit the ball consistently.

On guard with your weapon in hand at lunge distance away from the hanging ball. Extend your arm toward the ball, lunge, and hit the ball with the point of your weapon *before* your front foot lands on the floor. Return to on guard position. It is important to hit the ball before your foot lands because when your foot hits the floor your arm and your point move because of the impact.

**Success Goal =** Hit the ball 5 of 10 attempts____

## ✔ Success Check

- Relax shoulders____
- Start point first, extend smoothly____
- Keep your eyes always on the ball____
- Keep point steady and straight____
- Return always to on guard position before taking a break____

### To Increase Difficulty

- Use a ball the size of a tennis ball. Write numbers and letters on the ball. Call out the number or letter that you hit with your point.
- Stay on guard extension distance from the ball. Extend and hit the ball as it swings away from you, make a small lunge and hit the ball again.
- Use smaller ball.
- Hit the ball as it passes in front of you, while it is moving side to side.
- Hit the ball as it is swinging to and away from you.

### To Decrease Difficulty

- Use larger ball.
- Extend arm fully before you begin lunge.
- Shorten lunge.

### *3. Lunging at the Right Time*

On guard with your partner at short lunge distance (figure a). Your partner advances, you retreat (figure b). You both pause, you extend and lunge, hitting your partner in the shoulder area (figure c), recover back to on guard. You advance, your partner retreats, you both pause, your partner lunges and hits you in the shoulder area.

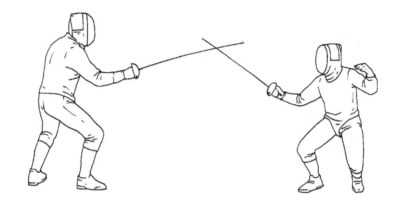

a

b

c

**Success Goal** = Repeat 10 series of the drill maintaining the lunge distance without having to take extra steps to adjust the distance____

### ✔ Success Check
- Relax shoulders____
- Move with your partner___
- Stay in low on guard___
- Start point first____
- Extend rear arm____
- Keep rear foot flat____
- Keep feet on an imaginary straight line____

### To Increase Difficulty
- Have partner raise rear hand when he wants you to lunge.
- Have partner say lunge when he wants you to lunge.
- Have partner bend his arm when he wants you to lunge.
- Move with your partner, advance two times and retreat two times before you lunge.

### To Decrease Difficulty
- Lunge from stationary position, eliminate footwork.
- Shorten the lunge.

## 4. Advance Lunge With Partner

On guard with your partner at a distance that you cannot hit with just a lunge. In other words, you must make an advance and a lunge to reach your partner. This is called advance lunge distance. Your partner advances two times and retreats three times; you follow but advance only twice. Your partner stops, you extend your weapon arm and make an advance lunge. Hit your partner in the shoulder area. You recover backward and retreat to your advance lunge distance.

**Success Goal** = Repeat the pattern 10 times without escaping from your on guard position____

### ✔ Success Check
- Relax shoulders____
- Move and keep distance with your partner___
- Keep your feet well placed under you in good balance____
- Extend your arm before you begin the advance lunge____
- Blade bends up as you hit____
- Leave your arm extended until after you have finished your backward recovery____

### To Increase Difficulty
- Designate two different spots on shoulder. Alternate hits.
- Hit thigh for epee.
- Hit bicep for epee. Partner's arm is bent.

### To Decrease Difficulty
- Hit with advance lunge, eliminate mobility.

### 5. Advance Lunge With a Very Calm Point

On guard at advance lunge distance from the ball hung from the ceiling at shoulder height. Extend your arm, advance lunge, hit the ball gently. Do not punch the ball. Remain in the lunge position, keep your point directed at the ball, move your point just enough to allow the swinging ball to swing back and hit your point. You must not poke at the ball. You must relax your shoulders and keep your point very calm. Allow the ball to come back toward you and place your point in line with the ball so it hits your point. This drill is not easy. To perform this drill you must relax and focus.

**Success Goal =** Hit the ball with the lunge and the rebound 8 times out of 20 tries____

**✔ Success Check**
- Relax your shoulders____
- Keep point steady____
- Check key positions of the lunge____
- Make a small advance____
- Return to on guard before you rest____

**To Increase Difficulty**
- Hit the ball with the lunge and the rebound 15 out of the 20 tries.
- Hit the ball with an advance lunge, recover from the lunge, and lunge again; front arm remains softly extended during the entire exercise.
- Advance and retreat before you advance lunge.

**To Decrease Difficulty**
- Hit the ball with the lunge, recover from the lunge backward, leave your arm extended, and hit the ball during one of the swings, not necessarily the first one.

---

## THRUST, LUNGE, AND RECOVERY SUCCESS SUMMARY

The thrust, lunge, and recovery from the lunge are the foundation of your fencing game. The attack and recovery from the attack test your reflexes and fearlessness. The thrust and lunge depend on your desire to hit and your recovery from the lunge depends on leg strength and mental flexibility, the ability to immediately switch from attack to defense. Balance, responsiveness, and flexibility are important physically, but the most important key to success is mental.

# STEP 4

## ENGAGEMENT AND CHANGE OF ENGAGEMENT: MAKING CONTACT WITH YOUR OPPONENT'S BLADE

Engagement is touching and maintaining light but firm contact with the opponent's weapon. Change of engagement is moving your blade from one side of the opponent's blade to the other, touching it lightly but firmly on the other side. The target area is broken up into four quadrants—inside and outside, high and low. When you change engagement you move from the inside to the outside line or from the high line to the low line, or a combination. The line refers to the quadrant of your opponent toward which your blade is pointing. You engage your opponent's blade so that your blade will be pointing at the quadrant of the target from which you wish to start. In fencing we recognize four quadrants—outside high, position 6; inside high, position 4; outside low, position 8; inside low, position 7. If your point is above your bell you are in high line. If your point is below your bell you are in low line.

you wish. From this simple tactile move you also can learn a great deal about your opponent and his tension level through the feel of his blade.

The change of engagement can be used to disturb your opponent, distract her from your true intentions, or hinder her from attacking. At the same time, you will search for ways to take advantage of her slightest mistake. There are a number of actions (offensive as well as defensive) that are initiated and developed from the change of engagement.

You will engage your opponent's blade and change engagement at the beginning of the bout to test your opponent's reactions, to determine his speed or technique, or to determine how tightly he is holding his weapon. This will give you hints regarding the choice of actions that will be most effective against him. In this step you will begin to learn to "read" your opponent.

## Why the Engagement and Change of Engagement Are Important

The engagement and the change of engagement are important because they help you develop precision, control, and maneuverability of your blade. You are also able to take or control the opponent's blade and to avoid your opponent's blade when

## How to Make an Engagement and Change of Engagement (Change the Line) in the High Line and Low Line

On guard facing your partner (figure 4.1a). To engage in the high line, the tip of your weapon should be higher than your bell. Your partner's tip is also

51

higher than her blade (figure 4.1b). Position yourself at a distance where you can engage (touch) your partner's blade with your arm about three-quarters extended (figure 4.1c). The partner's blade remains stationary while you move your blade from one side of the partner's blade to the other, slowly and precisely (figure 4.1d). Change engagement by moving your tip under the partner's blade using your fingers, not your wrist. Keep arm stationary and your wrist firm. Make your blade movement as small as possible. Touch the blade firmly on each side, pausing at each contact or engagement.

To engage in the low line both you and your partner's points must be below your bells (figure 4.2). Keep the same on guard hand position to engage in the low line, just drop the tips lower then the bells, with the tip pointing in the direction of your partner's thigh or knee. To change engagement in the low line move your tip over the top of your partner's blade instead of under it. Begin to feel with your blade as though it were a finger with an eye on the end. Your blade will begin to have a life of its own. You will begin to use your tactile sense and to educate your automatic reflexes to respond in a certain manner to particular tactile stimuli. Your response system will begin to act simultaneously with your decision-making process, thereby decreasing your reaction time. You will be performing the appropriate response before you are even aware of it.

<table>
<tr><td>**FIGURE 4.1**</td><td>**KEYS TO SUCCESS**</td></tr>
</table>

# ENGAGEMENT AND CHANGE OF ENGAGEMENT—HIGH LINE

a

b

## Preparation

1. On guard facing your partner___
2. Weapon arm is three-quarters extended___
3. Keep tips slightly higher than the bells___
4. Cross your blades about one-quarter of the way down the blade from the tip___

## Execution: Engagement

1. Engage partner's blade, pause___
2. Touch blade firmly___
3. Return to on guard, out of engagement (blades not touching) ___

## Execution: Change of Engagement

1. Engage partner's blade on one side___
2. Move your point in a very small circle underneath partner's blade___
3. Engage partner's blade on the other side of her blade lightly___
4. Bell remains stationary. Move only the tip of the blade using fingers___

### Follow-Up

5. Return to on guard position out of engagement___

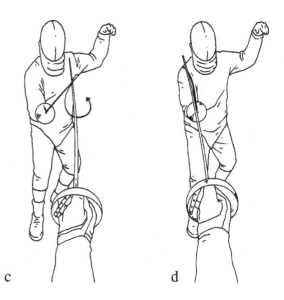

c          d

FIGURE 4.2 **KEYS TO SUCCESS**

# ENGAGEMENT AND CHANGE OF ENGAGEMENT—LOW LINE

### Preparation

1. On guard facing your partner___
2. Weapon arm is three-quarters extended___
3. Keep tips lower than the bells___
4. Cross your blades about one-quarter down the blade from the tip___

### Execution: Engagement

1 Engage your partner's blade, touching blades gently but firmly___
2. Pause; return arms to on guard___

### Execution: Change of Engagement

1. Engage partner's blade on one side___
2. Move your point in a very small circle above partner's blade___
3. Lightly engage partner's blade on the other side of his blade___
4. Keep bell stationary. Move only the tip of the blade using your fingers___

### Follow-Up

1. Return arms to on guard position, out of engagement___

The ability to contact your opponent's blade is critical, particularly in foil. Contacting your opponent's blade with confidence and allowing your opponent to contact your blade without fear of consequences allows you to relax and move on the strip with freedom and force. You do not have this relaxed confidence if you are afraid of blade contact. Fear on the fencing strip causes many problems. Some fencers are distracted by opponents touching their blade. Practicing engagements will help you become more confident with blade contact and help you learn to control the opponent's blade.

| Error | Correction |
|---|---|
| 1. Contacting the partner's blade too harshly or changing engagement too quickly. | 1. Slowly move your point first to partner's blade. Move slowly, changing the line. Touch the blade with the question "What can I learn from this blade?" Move your point with your fingers. |
| 2. Moving the blade in too large an arc using your arm and wrist. | 2. Try to make an arc no larger than your partner's bell, as small as possible. Keep your wrist firm. Maneuver the point with your fingers. |
| 3. Dropping the bell and arm too much to engage in the low line. | 3. Keep bell almost the same level as in the on guard position, but drop the point to engage in low line. Move the tip from high line to low line focusing on the bell moving very little. |

## ENGAGEMENT AND CHANGE OF ENGAGEMENT

# DRILLS

Throughout these drills I will explain the drills to you and your partner. Your partner will be expected to keep constant distance in most situations—if you advance, your partner will retreat to maintain the predetermined distance—advance distance, lunge distance, for instance, as you move on the strip. The person following will be responsible for the control of the correct distance; sometimes you will be following. Your partner will always keep a good on guard position with point slightly up in the high line and slightly down toward the thigh, in the low line, so you are able to engage his blade and perform the described action. It may be necessary for the partner to move his weapon slightly to allow you to touch the target. Your partner should not block your touch or retreat so far away that you cannot touch on the determined action. During the drills your partner assumes an aggressive posture. If the drill calls for you to press on the blade, the pressure is firm but the point should not move very much.

While keeping distance do not move your arm in and out; to adjust for the change of distance, use your legs. If you move your arm to maintain the perception of correct distance your partner or opponent can easily be within distance to score a touch on you before you can react. Make your legs move to stay at the correct distance.

Your partner's responsibility in the pair drills is to give you the ideal situation to perform the change of engagement or other specified action. Your partner helps you perform the action correctly. It is very easy to make it hard for a person to do a drill, but it is extremely difficult to focus and do the right action at both the right time and distance to allow the fencer doing the drill to be able to perform the action correctly.

Begin the blade engagement from either side of the blade and in the next action start the engagement from the other side of the blade. Your partner may need to move his blade slightly or bend his arm a little to allow you to touch. This assistance should not be exaggerated.

To prepare for these drills place a piece of tape on your blade about 20 to 30 centimeters (8 to 12 inches) from the point. The tape width should be 3 or 4 centimeters (1 or 1.5 inches). Some of these drills will make use of this tape to help you identify your distance.

## 1. Controlled Bouting With Engagement

Get on guard with your partner, in lunge distance and engage blades. You (as the leader) advance and retreat, and your partner must keep correct distance. When bouting, you never look at the blades but at the shoulders or head with a soft focus. Some great fencers have even been known to look at the hip area. The leader tries to touch when the distance is too close by an advance or a lunge. Even though one may try as hard as she can to keep the correct distance, it is sometimes very short. The distance becomes too short because someone makes a mistake. This is the moment when touches can be scored. Janusz Peciak, Olympic Gold Medalist and Olympic coach, often explains that fencing is a game of mistakes, and the one who makes the fewest mistakes wins. We are focusing here on the concept of the bout, how to score, and how to keep from being scored on. The leader tries to close distance with rapid footwork, and the partner tries to keep the correct distance to avoid being hit. The leader cannot take more than three advances or three retreats in a row without changing direction. Touches are scored not by chasing your opponent down but by forcing him to change direction often. An ideal time to score on your opponent is when he stops retreating and begins to come forward. The opponent is at a slight disadvantage at this moment.

Do not beat your partner's blade to defend yourself; retreat when you see the attack coming. You must use your legs to defend yourself. Be smart and remember what is successful. Repeat what is successful.

**Success Goal** = 8 sets of 30-second bouts with 30 seconds rest. The leader must score at least one point each 30 seconds____

### Success Check
- Relax shoulders____
- Keep arm three-quarters extended, press the arm forward ready to extend and touch____
- Keep arm in good on guard position____
- Do not bend your arm to maintain distance, use your legs____
- Focus on the distance between you and your partner____

### To Increase Difficulty
- Increase time to 45 seconds.
- Do 12 sets of 30-second bouts with 30 seconds rest in between.

### To Decrease Difficulty
- Move on the strip but do not try to score.
- You lead and if the distance becomes too short, you stop until your partner repairs the distance.

## 2A. High-Line Change of Engagement, Attack With Advance

On guard facing partner in advance distance. You engage in the high line with the tape touching. You change engagement two times, pause with each engagement. You extend, advance, and touch partner in chest, (partner remains stationary) recover backward to on guard position at advance distance. This is one set.

**Success Goal =** 25 sets. Hit same spot on partner's chest_____

### ✔ Success Check

- Keep arm in proper on guard position_____
- Move point first using your fingers_____
- Hold engagement firmly_____
- Make thrust before you advance to target_____
- Begin advance as you finish extension; make it all one continuous move_____
- For epee, raise bell slightly higher than the point as you touch, keep level for foil_____

### To Increase Difficulty

- Do drill from lunge distance and lunge to touch partner.
- Add mobility before change of engagement and hit.
- Remain in on guard during the 25 sets.
- Accelerate to the hit.

### To Decrease Difficulty

- Stay engaged longer.
- Do each part of the action separately.
- Decrease the number of sets.

## 2B. High-Line Change of Engagement With Lunge (You Lead)

On guard facing partner in lunge distance. Engage in high line touching the tape you put on your blades earlier. You change engagement, advance, change engagement, retreat, thrust and lunge, touch partner on his chest. Your partner must keep distance by following your footwork. Partner does not retreat when you lunge but allows you to hit. Try to touch tape to tape each time you change engagement. Be sure to change engagement before you move your feet. This is one set.

**Success Goal =** 10 sets. Touch partner on same spot on chest_____

### ✔ Success Check

- Keep arm three-quarters extended in proper on guard position_____
- Keep trunk steady and straight_____
- Keep point movement small. Make change of engagement using only the point_____
- Straighten rear arm and rear leg in the lunge; hold this position momentarily before you recover_____

### To Increase Difficulty

- Change engagement, then double advance, pause, extend, and lunge, touching your partner on his chest. Your partner does not retreat when you lunge but allows you to hit. Your partner must move with you to stay at lunge distance.
- Change engagement, then double retreat, pause, extend, and lunge, touching your partner on his chest.
- Change the amount of pressure on your partner's blade.

### To Decrease Difficulty

- Do each element of the action separately.

### 2C. High-Line Change of Engagement With Lunge (Partner Leads)

On guard with your partner at lunge distance. Engage in the high line with pressure. You follow as your partner advances two times, you retreat two times and change engagement after last retreat. Then your partner retreats one time and you change engagement and advance. Your partner presses on your blade slightly, you change engagement, thrust, and lunge to the target. Touch your partner on the chest and pause in the lunge (figure b). Recover backward to on guard, repair the distance, and continue the drill from lunge distance.

**Success Goal** = 10 sets. Touch the partner on the same spot on his chest with your thrust____

a

### Success Check

- Relax shoulders____
- Keep arm three-quarters extended____
- Make small advances and retreats____
- Sit in a low on guard position____
- Begin extension of your point to target before you lunge____
- Recover to on guard position without dropping your point or bell____

### To Increase Difficulty

- Have your partner press your blade as a cue for you to make each change of engagement.
- Do the drill from advance lunge distance; hit with an advance lunge.

### To Decrease Difficulty

- You lead the exercise. Your partner must respond to you as you retreat and change engagement, you advance, then your partner presses on your blade and you change engagement and lunge.

b

### 3A. Low-Line Change of Engagement

On guard facing your partner in advance distance. Engage in low line touching tape to tape. You change engagement two times, hold engagement firmly, pause for one second, then release partner's blade, extend toward your partner's chest, advance, and touch your partner. Be sure to move your point first. Return to on guard position. Your partner remains in on guard position. (For epee, you may select another target.)

**Success Goal** = 10 sets without break.
Hit your partner on the same spot on the chest___

**Success Check**
- Relax___
- Keep your trunk steady and straight___
- Do not drop bell to engage___
- Move your point over the top of your partner's blade using your fingers___
- Press point forward when you change engagement___
- Extend your arm before your advance___

**To Increase Difficulty**
- Perform the drill with a lunge from your lunge distance.
- Mark two areas on your partner's chest and alternate hitting the two spots.

**To Decrease Difficulty**
- Do each action separately.

### 3B. Low-Line Change of Engagement With Lunge

On guard with your partner at lunge distance (figure a). Your partner makes two advances, you keep distance. Your partner presses on your blade firmly, you change engagement then direct point toward chest (figure b), thrust, and lunge to your partner's chest (figure c).

Recover back to on guard and adjust distance to the original lunge distance.

Next, your partner retreats two times, you keep distance, change engagement after your last advance, thrust, and lunge, touching partner on chest. Recover back to on guard position. This is one set (for epee, you may choose other target areas as shown in figure d).

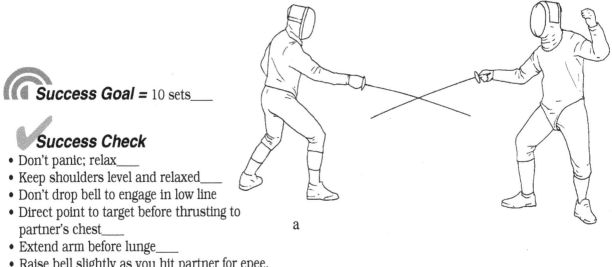

a

**Success Goal** = 10 sets___

**Success Check**
- Don't panic; relax___
- Keep shoulders level and relaxed___
- Don't drop bell to engage in low line___
- Direct point to target before thrusting to partner's chest___
- Extend arm before lunge___
- Raise bell slightly as you hit partner for epee, keep level for foil___

b

c

d

## 4. Thrust From Engagement in the High Line

On guard in advance distance with your partner. Engage your partner's blade in high line. You change engagement and advance, pause, partner changes engagement, pause, you change engagement and retreat. Then you thrust and hit your partner with an advance. Retreat back to advance distance. This is one set.

**Success Goal** = 25 sets. Thrust to same spot on partner's chest____

**Success Check**
• Stay in low on guard position____
• Start point first and make movements smoothly____
• Keep trunk steady____
• At moment of touch, the bell should be slightly higher than the point in epee. The point and bell are the same level for foil ____

**To Increase Difficulty**
• Advance and retreat before change of engagement, your partner keeping distance.
• Advance two times before change of engagement, your partner keeping distance.

**To Decrease Difficulty**
• Slow down drill and perform each part separately.

## 5. Combination Attacking With a Lunge

On guard in advance distance facing your partner. Engage your partner's blade in the low line (figure a), you advance, your partner retreats keeping distance. Your partner raises her blade to high line and advances (figure b), you engage in high line (figure c) and retreat, keeping distance. Your partner releases your blade by dropping her point down and away from your blade and makes a small retreat. You lunge. Your lunge should be short and correct (figure d). Recover back into a perfect on guard position and regain advance distance. This is one set.

a          b

c          d

Success Goal = 10 sets. Hit the same spot on partner's chest____

### Success Check
- Complete blade work before you move your feet____
- Take small steps____
- Extend your arm before you begin the lunge____
- Straighten your rear arm during the lunge____
- Kick out with the front foot in the lunge____
- Recover to on guard position with your feet at correct distance____

### To Increase Difficulty
- Hit in exactly the same spot each time.
- Increase the acceleration to the target.
- Add 10 seconds of footwork before each set.

### To Decrease Difficulty
- Pause after each set.
- Do each action separately.

## 6. Response to Opponent's Pressure in the High Line and Low Line

On guard with your partner in advance distance. Engage blades in high line, your partner will move from high line to low line when she chooses and you must follow. Your partner advances or retreats as she wishes and you must follow and keep distance; when your partner gently but firmly presses your blade, you change engagement. You only change engagement in response to partner's pressure; stay in contact with partner's blade and keep correct distance.

**Success Goal =** 4 × 30 seconds work × 30 seconds rest____

### Success Check

• Use your fingers to maneuver your blade____
• Respond quickly and smoothly to your partner's pressure____
• Move the point as little as possible____
• Respond only after your partner's pressure____
• Don't anticipate____
• Be alert____

### To Increase Difficulty

• Try this drill with your eyes closed, responding to your partner's pressure and trying to keep distance. This is a challenge but will heighten your sensitivity.
• Extend and lunge, hitting your partner in chest each time he presses your blade when you advance.
• Extend and lunge, hitting your partner in chest each time he presses your blade when you retreat.
• Extend and lunge, hitting your partner in chest each time he removes his blade away from yours.

### To Decrease Difficulty

• Do drill moving only in one direction.
• Do drill only in high line and then only in low line.
• Predetermine the footwork pattern.
• Do each action separately.
• Partner tells you when to change engagement.

## ENGAGEMENT AND CHANGE OF ENGAGEMENT SUCCESS SUMMARY

One of the marks of a complete fencer is his ability to analyze his opponent and test his reactions to various stimuli to determine the appropriate course of action to follow during the bout, as well as to understand his own reactions to those stimuli as his opponent tests him. The more you practice the drills in this step, the more comfortable you will be in knowing "what to do next." Your opponent is giving you the information by his responses to your engagements, changes of engagement, and response to pressure.

Before learning how to execute high-line offensive moves in the next step, have your partner or coach check the Keys to Success engagement and change of engagement skills for the high line illustrated in figure 4.1. The key to the use of the attacks lies in being ready to attack: maintaining your balance; keeping visual and tactile focus on your opponent; and responding quickly, but without guessing.

# STEP 5

## PARRY-RIPOSTE HIGH LINE: TURNING THE TIDE

The high-line parries that we will discuss in this step are parry 4 and parry 6. A high-line parry defends against a threat to the area above the hips. The parry is a defensive blade maneuver made to deflect the blade of the attacker away from the target. Although the first way to defend yourself in fencing is to move away with the feet, the parry, the second way to protect your target can be taken while the feet are moving backward, standing still, or even moving forward.

The parry is used often in both foil and epee. The foil parry needs to protect the trunk while the epee parry must protect the entire body. Other means of defense include the counterattack and evasive body actions, such as ducks, bends, and turns that cause your opponent to miss. The counterattack in epee is a thrust to the nearest unprotected target during an opponent's attack. The counterattack is a valuable weapon to use as your opponent begins to create his attack. Hit early and often. In foil, you may counter attack, but you must be sure your opponent does not hit you because he has right of way.

The parry is used to avoid being hit, and the riposte is the action made by the defender to score a touch after successfully parrying the attack. The purpose of the parry is not fully served unless you can turn the tide and score with the riposte. Parry 4 protects the inside line (the front of the torso), while the parry 6 protects the outside line (shoulder and, especially in foil, the back).

## Why Is the Parry-Riposte Important?

The parry-riposte is an action done to prevent your opponent from hitting you and also to enable you to score. It is the second line of defense and is a high percentage scoring maneuver. Beginning and intermediate fencers all over the world attack first and think second. Some fencers may lose patience and attack; others attack out of fear, the fear of being hit or the fear of not knowing what else to do. You must learn very early how to defend yourself, or your opponent has little reason not to attack you whenever she wants.

The parry-riposte allows you to move toward the intermediate and advanced levels of fencing. It should be an integral part of your game and not just used in desperation to avoid being hit. If you have weak parries and ripostes you can expect your opponent to make numerous attacks against your undefended or poorly defended position. Once you become confident that you can parry most (or at least some) attacks and riposte with authority, the level of your game is greatly improved. A good parry-riposte can have a demoralizing effect on the attacking fencer. Fencing is a game of wits, and if you can short-circuit your opponent's confidence, thereby inhibiting his ability to function at full capacity, you will have a tremendous weapon at your fingertips. Make your opponent doubt or question himself and the ball is in your court. You have the momentum.

The parry and the riposte are two independent phases of one action. One can continually parry, but unless it is paired with the riposte your opponent will keep attacking since she faces no threat of being hit. In most circumstances you want to follow the parry with an immediate riposte.

For foil fencers the parry ends the attack of the opponent. The right-of-way rule gives the defender the priority to score immediately, even if the attacking opponent continues and hits first with a remise (a continuation of the attack after being parried).

Epee has no right-of-way rule, so the touch must be scored by time alone. You must hit your opponent 1/25 of a second before he hits you to score a point. The parry in epee is for practical purposes. It gives you time to try to score a point before your opponent can continue and hit you. Whoever hits first gets the point. In epee, the purpose of the parry is to move the blade so you are not hit. In foil, the purpose is to gain right of way.

### When Is a Good Time to Parry?

The best time to parry the attack of most opponents is the moment the attack begins, before it is fully developed. The parry at the end of the attack, just before the opponent hits your target, is the time most parries are made and is the second-best alternative. A fencer is vulnerable at the time of full extension in his attack, at the very end of the attack. It is similar to a football player being fully stretched out to catch a pass. He has no defenses.

# How to Execute a Parry in the High Line

The spanking parry is the beating of the opponent's blade done defensively. It is a crisp beat done on the attacking blade. There are as many acceptable ways to make parries and ripostes as there are countries in the fencing world and as many variations on these actions as there are fencers and coaches, but the basics are always the same. Additionally, the degree of extension of the weapon arm will vary, depending on the distance you are from your opponent when you parry. A vitally important aspect of the parry is the time you parry and the distance from which you parry. In foil, ideally, you will reach slightly forward and parry

the attacking blade the instant the attack begins. In epee you can do the same action, but the bell moves toward the opponent's blade and blocks the opponent's blade from hitting you as your arm reaches full extension, called a closing parry. It is not always possible to parry at this time; sometimes in epee you need to bring your bell back slightly for the classic parry and move your bell toward the opponent's blade, creating a blocking action. Remember you always move the point of the blade first.

The least effective time to parry is in the middle of the opponent's attack because the opponent has time and distance to avoid the parry. Most of the time you should retreat when you parry to give yourself enough distance to have time to parry before you are hit. But there are times when you may be standing still, moving back, or even moving forward when you parry.

# How to Execute a Parry 4

The parry 4 is used to deflect the blade of the attacker when the opponent attacks to your chest. The parry is made by moving your blade from the on guard position across your body laterally (figure 5.1a). The tip moves first, followed immediately with hand and forearm, all reaching the parry position together (figure 5.1b). The wrist and forearm snap the blade in a small but dynamic arc toward your opponent's blade (figure 5.1c). The arm extends slightly, reaching for the attacking blade. (As in soccer you must attack the ball when receiving a pass.) If you parry late in the attack when the point is near your chest, you may need to bring the bell back to block the attack. The hand rotates slightly in the direction of the attacking blade. The wrist may change position slightly (depending on the distance at which you are parrying) but must be held firmly. After the parry your blade moves to thrusting position pointing toward your opponent's target, prepared for the next action.

**FIGURE 5.1**

## KEYS TO SUCCESS

# PARRY 4

a

b

c

## Preparation

1. On guard with opponent in advance distance___
2. Opponent thrusts toward your chest from lunge distance ___

## Execution

1. Parry by moving your tip first, then hand and forearm in one continuous movement___
2. Arm slightly extends as you parry if you parry early in the attack. If you parry late, the arm bends and brings the bell back to parry 6___

3. Move your blade in an arc across your chest, contacting your opponent's blade

    ___
4. Bell finishes slightly lower than in on guard position

    ___
5. Keep elbow inside ___

## Follow-Up

1. Return immediately to on guard position ___
2. Be prepared for next maneuver ___

## SUCCESS STOPPERS

The most critical error in parrying is not being prepared for the attack. The fencer does not keep correct distance, and when an attack comes, she is not ready, thereby making the response in panic, sometimes choosing the wrong action, making the parry too early, too late, or too large.

| Error | Correction |
|---|---|
| 1. Moving bell first and making the movement too large. | 1. Move point first and stop when you contact opponent's blade, or if you do not contact blade, stop in correct parry 4 position and immediately return to on guard position. |
| 2. Holding grip too tightly or too loosely. | 2. Hold firmly enough to control blade and loosely enough to manipulate the point with the fingers. |
| 3. Making parry too hard and dropping point below bell guard, sometimes hitting the floor. | 3. Make parry slowly and smoothly, control each movement. Blade finishes at about a 30- to 45-degree angle above the bell guard. |
| 4. Moving elbow around. | 4. Stabilize your elbow. |

# How to Execute Parry 6

The parry 6 is a movement of the blade to defend against an attack directed to the forward shoulder and chest in foil, while in epee you protect the arm, shoulder, chest, and head. The parry starts in the on guard position at advance distance and is done by moving the blade and arm laterally and by slightly raising your point (figures 5.2a and b). The tip of the weapon is higher than the bell, and it is the first to move, followed immediately with the hand and forearm, all reaching the parry position together. The wrist is held firmly, and the forearm muscles contract forcefully. The elbow must be stabilized and inside toward the body. The arm extends slightly and the hand rotates outward a little (clockwise for right-handed, counterclockwise for left-handed). The bell is about midbiceps high.

Epee fencers must contact the opponent's blade with the intent of not allowing the opponent's point to hit, even after the parry. To score a point the defending epee fencer must hit the opponent with the riposte 1/25 of a second before the attacker hits him. Without the opponent scoring otherwise, it will be called a double touch if both fencers hit at the same time and both fencers score.

**FIGURE
5.2**

**KEYS TO SUCCESS**

# PARRY 6

## Preparation

1. On guard with opponent in advance distance___
2. Your weapon is in 4 position___
3. Opponent thrusts to your 6 line ___

a

b

## Execution

1. Move tip first, then hand and forearm, all finishing together ___
2. Move tip laterally in a small clockwise arc to contact blade firmly (counterclockwise for left-handed) ___

3. Extend slightly as you parry ___
4. Keep elbow in toward body ___
5. Finish with point slightly outside the opponent's body line ___

## Follow-Up

1. Return to on guard position ___

The parry 6 is a great defensive weapon. The main problem is that the pant of the weapon does not move first. Many fencers find it difficult to move to the parry 6 position quickly and efficiently. If the elbow moves out before the point moves, an opponent is able to hit you before your blade and bell blocks their attack.

| Error | Correction |
|---|---|
| 1. Not moving the tip first to parry but breaking the wrist and moving the bell or elbow first. | 1. The wrist is held firmly to create a straight line from the elbow to the point. The blade movement is done with the fingers. Control the movement precisely. Focus on moving the point first and holding wrist firmly. |
| 2. Bringing the bell back toward the shoulder, panicked. | 2. Move the point up and slightly forward as you parry. |
| 3. Parrying too late or too early, frenzied. | 3. Make the parry as the opponent extends arm to hit you and is within your distance to parry. Focus on distance and timing. |

## Circle Parries

Circle parries are important when you find your blade on the wrong side of the opponent's blade for you to use the parry you have chosen. The circle parry also protects more of your target from your opponent's attacks.

## How to Execute a Circle Parry 4

You make the change of engagement, but you must move the opponent's blade away from your target area. Engage opponent's blade in your 6. Make a change of engagement and firmly contact the opponent's blade. You do not have to be engaged in 6. You may perform circle parry from out of engagement (figure 5.3).

**FIGURE 5.3** **KEYS TO SUCCESS**

# CIRCULAR PARRY 4

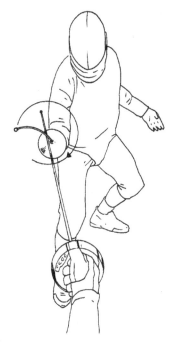

a

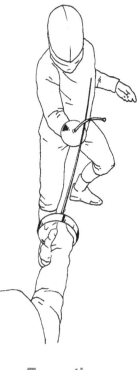

b

c

### Preparation

1. On guard with opponent in advance distance__
2. Engage opponent's blade in your 6__

### Execution

1. Change engagement contacting opponent's blade firmly on the other side__
2. Blade moves in a counter-clockwise direction (for right-handed) with point moving first__

### Follow-Up

1. Return to on guard position __

## How to Make a Circle Parry 6

The circle parry 6 is necessary for protecting yourself when the opponent attacks you high in your front shoulder area. The change of engagement moving clockwise for a right-handed fencer gives you the direction and the movement of the circle parry 6. Be sure the point moves first and stays above your bell about eye level (figure 5.4a). The muscles used in this parry are usually weaker than the muscles you use to do a parry 4, so be sure the tip moves first and contacts the attacking blade as quickly and firmly as possible (figure 5.4b). Contact blade firmly, moving opponent's blade away from your target (figure 5.4c). Your tip is slightly outside the line of the opponent's body on contact. It is very important that the arm extends slightly if the parry is early and retracts slightly if the parry is late. Immediately after the parry, riposte immediately by thrusting to the target.

**FIGURE 5.5** **KEYS TO SUCCESS**

# CIRCLE PARRY 6

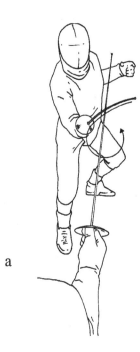

a

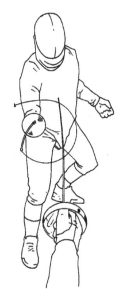

b

## Preparation

1. On guard with opponent in extension distance___
2. Engage opponent's blade in 4 or from out of engagement ___

## Execution

1. Move point first, dropping it under the opponent's blade ___
2. Keep your tip higher than your bell, about eye level___
3. Continue in semicircle like the change of engagement ___
4. Keep your wrist firm ___
5. Your tip, bell, and forearm reach final position simultaneously ___

## Follow-Up

1. Return to on guard position ___

c

## SUCCESS STOPPERS

When using circle parries it is important to control your blade, not using your arm, but mainly the fingers, keeping the parry small. The circular movement must be fluid and should stop at the end of the circle. Do not chase opponent's blade if it is wild and out of position. The movement must be done primarily with the fingers, with a slight movement of the wrist, keeping the body steady.

| Error | Correction |
|---|---|
| 1. Making parry too large. | 1. Move point in a small circular motion using your fingers. Tighten forearm forcefully and lock your wrist to stop blade movement. |
| 2. Using arm and shoulder to execute action. | 2. Move tip first using your fingers. Allow wrist to move slightly. Keep shoulder down, do not allow it to rise up and tighten. |
| 3. Raising elbow out to the side. | 3. Press your elbow inside and pointed toward the floor. |

## How to Execute the Riposte

The riposte is the offensive maneuver made after you parry. Most of the time you riposte, by thrusting directly to the target immediately after the parry. If you need your riposte to be more precise after you parry, return your blade to thrusting position (the forearm and blade are parallel to floor), and then thrust. This can be used only for foil. The point of the weapon must move first toward the target.

Most ripostes for foil are made to the high line (shoulder) area. The foil target area is very small—you must hit the lame. The riposte for epee may be to the hand, biceps area, shoulder, mask, thigh, or lower leg. Time is of the essence. Remember—you must have 1/25 of second advantage over your opponent, thereby creating the necessity for hitting the nearest target.

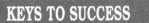

FIGURE
5.3    **KEYS TO SUCCESS**

# RIPOSTE

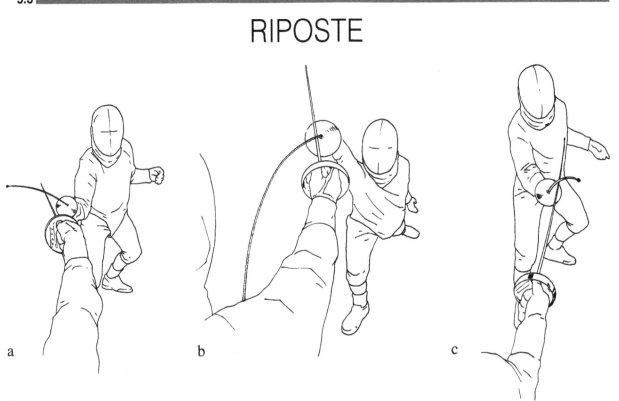

a                    b                    c

## Preparation

1. On guard with opponent in extension distance___
2. Opponent thrusts ___
3. Parry (4 or 6) ___

## Execution

1. Thrust directly to target after the parry ___
2. Move point first, using fingers ___
3. Keep shoulder relaxed and down ___
4. Raise bell slightly as you hit for epee; for foil, bell stays at same level___

## Follow-Up

1. After your riposte, return immediately to on guard position ___
2. Retreat out of distance ___

## SUCCESS STOPPERS

You must riposte directly after the parry without pausing. Many people hold the parry and do not riposte because they feel safe when holding the opponent's blade. You must parry with the intention of hitting your opponent not just to defend yourself—you parry to score a touch.

| Error | Correction |
|---|---|
| 1. Punching the riposte or moving the body first. | 1. Move point first continuously to target immediately after parry. Do not move body. |
| 2. Not riposting immediately and holding the parry. | 2. As soon as you parry, press your point forward to hit. The riposte is an attack—move the blade aggressively. |
| 3. Moving bell guard or elbow. | 3. Thrust the point forward. After you make the parry, feel as though something were holding your hand back and suddenly released it. The point explodes forward like a rubber band pulled too tightly and then released. |

## PARRY-RIPOSTE HIGH LINE

# DRILLS

Your partner's responsibility during the drills is to make a thrust that you can parry, extending slowly for you to have time to do the required defensive action. When the distance is close, your partner may need to do a one-half to three-quarters extension. Thrusting from the same position each time will increase your accuracy dramatically. It is necessary for your partner to allow easy access to the target.

Take each of the blade actions—parry 4, parry 6, circle parry 4, circle parry 6—and practice with each of the following footwork actions: stationary, retreat, retreat-advance, retreat-lunge. Take one parry through all the footwork drills before moving to the next parry. Timing and coordination of each parry and footwork will be discussed below. If this is too unwieldy for you at this time, do each parry from the stationary position.

Drills are used to refine skills. Do the drills slowly and methodically to perfect precise muscle memorization of each action. Speed will increase as your technique, timing, and distance improve. Excellent fencing skills come from correct repetition of the simple maneuvers. Master the basics!

Repeat the designated drills with each of the following footwork combinations.

- Extension distance—You and your partner are stationary __
- Extension distance—You retreat when your partner thrusts and advances __
- Advance distance—You retreat and parry when your partner thrusts and advances, then you thrust and advance to hit with riposte__
- Lunge distance—You retreat and parry when your partner thrusts and advances, then you thrust and lunge with riposte __

## 1. Parry 4

On guard in extension distance with your partner. Your partner's blade is below your bell, your partner raises his point to your inside line to eye level, you do a parry 4, and riposte directly. When adding the footwork, return to on guard position after the hit and retreat into correct distance, ready for the next action.

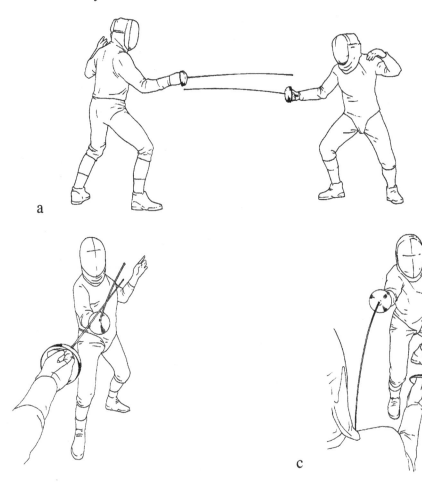

a

b

c

![checkmark icon] **Success Goal =** Hit opponent in the same spot on chest 5 times with each footwork pattern without dropping your point or bell below your waist at any time during the drill ___

### Success Check

- Partner's point must be higher than your bell for you to parry 4 ___
- Keep your tip above your bell ___
- Start point first and move the bell very little when making the parry ___
- Keep your wrist straight and solid. Parry the attacking blade firmly ___
- Use fingers to control the blade ___
- Begin your thrust before you move your feet___

### To Increase Difficulty

- Partner thrusts faster and changes rhythm of thrusts.
- Partner beats your blade before thrusting.
- You follow as your partner leads unpatterned footwork.

### To Decrease Difficulty

- Hold parry position for one second before riposting.
- Partner holds his blade in on guard position, in your 4, and you parry the blade when you choose.
- Do each action separately.

## 2. Circle Parry 4

Do the circle parry 4 drill with the following four variations with each of the prior footwork combinations. The actions are the same, but the cues to begin the actions are different.

1. Get on guard facing your partner at extension distance. Engage your partner's blade in 6 position. Do a circle parry 4 and riposte.
2. Engage your partner's blade in 4 position, your partner then makes a change of engagement but does not touch your blade, he extends into your 6 line instead of touching your blade. You make your circle parry 4 in response to your partner's extension and then riposte.
3. Get on guard facing your partner in advance distance. Your partner extends toward your chest. You make a slow parry 4, your partner changes engagement at the moment before you touch her blade, and then she thrusts without touching your blade on the 6 line of your blade. You continue your parry 4 into a circle parry 4 and contact your partner's blade on the other side and riposte. You and your partner will need to do the action very slowly.

**Success Goal =** Complete each of the three actions with each of the footwork patterns five times, hitting shoulder area in the same place each time ___

### Success Check

- Start each action from the correct on guard position ___
- Stop your blade when in correct 4 position___
- Focus on the distance between you and your training partner before the action begins___
- Retreat back to correct distance, remain in on guard position, ready for the next action ___

### To Increase Difficulty

- Increase speed and change rhythm of action.
- Make actions continuous by retreating after each riposte to correct distance; proceed immediately with the next action.
- Increase number of repetitions.
- Bounce during preparation for action.
- Let partner lead the footwork and you follow. Your partner gives you a cue (either vocal or with the blade) to begin your action.

### To Decrease Difficulty

- Practice on a stationary target instead of your partner.
- Break action into individual parts; perform each action slowly.

### *3. Parry 6*

Get on guard facing your partner at extension distance. Move your body laterally so the front feet of both you and your partner are directly in line. The lateral movement of your on guard position is only to make this drill easier for your partner to thrust to your 6 line and for you to riposte. Your partner must bend his arm, returning his arm to on guard position to allow you to hit. Weapon arm should be three quarters extended before the initiation of foot movement and fully extended for epee. The coordination should be smooth and continuous. Riposte as your partner returns his arm to on guard position.

Engage partner's blade in 4 position (a). You press gently on your partner's blade. This is your partner's cue to change the line and thrust to your 6 line without touching your blade (b). You parry 6 (c) and riposte to your partner's shoulder (d). Your partner must return his arm to on guard for you to riposte.

**Success Goal =** Repeat drill 3 with each of the prior footwork combinations 5 times, hitting partner in same spot on shoulder with riposte ___

### Success Check

• Beat or spank the blade as you parry in foil ___
• For epee move your bell a little more to block partner's blade ___
• Stop your weapon upon contact with your partner's blade ___
• Begin your thrust to target before footwork ___
• Accelerate the last part of the riposte ___

### To Increase Difficulty

• Increase speed and change rhythm.
• Make actions continuous.
• Increase number of repetitions.
• Bounce during preparation for action.
• Riposte to different spots on your partner.

### To Decrease Difficulty

• Practice on a stationary target instead of a training partner.
• Reduce number of repetitions.
• Break the action into separate parts and perform slowly.

## 4. Circle Parry 6

Perform the following circle parry 6 drills with each of the footwork drill sequences on page 73.

4.1 Engage training partner's blade in 4 position. Initiate your circle parry 6 with no cue from your partner.

4.2 You respond to a cue given by your partner. Engage your partner in 6 position. Your partner changes engagement and without touching your blade thrusts into your 4 line. You make your circle parry 6 in response to your partner's extension and then riposte.

4.3 You initiate the action by engaging in the 6 position and from this position press your partner's blade. In response to your pressure your partner changes engagement and thrusts into your 4 line without touching your blade. Your pressure should be just enough to provoke a response from your partner. Your partner should be very responsive and sensitive to the slightest pressure on her blade. You make your circle parry 6 in response and then riposte.

4.4 Get on guard facing your partner in extension distance. Your partner thrusts over your bell toward your shoulder, you move to parry 6, and your partner changes engagement before you touch her blade and thrusts to your shoulder without touching your blade. You continue your parry 6 into a circle parry 6, contacting your partner's blade, then riposte. You and your partner will need to do the drill slowly at first.

**Success Goal** = Repeat actions 4.1-4.4 with each of the prior footwork combinations on page 73 five times each, hitting the designated target area each time. ___

**Success Check**
- Keep circle small when you do the circle parry 6 using only point___
- Stop your weapon upon contact with your partner's weapon ___
- Return to on guard position after each parry riposte___
- Begin extension to target before foot movement ___

**To Increase Difficulty**
- Increase speed and rhythm.
- Do advances and retreats in no particular pattern before you start each action.
- Increase number of repetitions.
- Bounce during preparation for action.

**To Decrease Difficulty**
- Practice on a stationary target instead of a partner.
- Do each part of the action separately and slowly.
- Break after each action.

### 5. Parry and Thrust for Distance Awareness

In this drill you will practice maintaining distance as your partner moves on the fencing strip. Your partner will attack you with a lunge. (Your partner may stay in the lunge, recover forward, or recover backward as his part of the drill.) You must retreat and parry (using one of the parries you have just learned) and then thrust toward your partner, but do not move your feet to cover the distance to hit. Stop after your thrust with your arm still extended toward your partner; look at the distance between you and your partner. Visually measure and tell your partner what footwork is necessary for you to hit, then do the footwork to see if you have judged correctly. For epee, you may hit knee.

a

b

c

**Success Goal =** Judge the distance and choose the correct footwork necessary to cover this distance to hit 8 of 10 tries ___

### Success Check
- Move with your partner, maintaining same distance___

### To Increase Difficulty
- Have partner use fast footwork, changing length of steps.
- Have partner change direction often.
- Have partner change rhythm and speed.

### To Decrease Difficulty
- You lead the footwork.
- Have the partner change direction slowly when he leads.

Footwork variations and detailed progression:

1. Get on guard at extension distance with training partner. Remain in stationary position, your partner thrusts, and you parry and riposte without either of you moving your feet. Your partner's thrust must be done slowly and only one-half to three-quarters extension.
2. Get on guard at advance distance from your partner. Your partner thrusts and advances. You parry and riposte from stationary position.
3. Get on guard at lunge distance from your partner. Your partner thrusts and lunges. You parry and riposte from stationary on guard position.
4. Get on guard at extension distance from your partner. Your partner thrusts and advances, you retreat and parry, and then riposte.
5. Get on guard at lunge distance from your partner. Your partner thrusts and advances, you retreat and parry, and then thrust and lunge to hit your partner.
6. Get on guard at advance distance from your partner. Your partner thrusts and lunges, you retreat, parry, and then riposte while your partner is in the lunge.
7. Get on guard at lunge distance from your partner. Your partner thrusts and lunges, you retreat at the same time and parry, and then you lunge with your riposte as your partner recovers backward from his lunge into an on guard position.

It may make it easier to measure your drill distances by marking them on the floor until you visually memorize the distances: extension distance, advance distance, and lunge distance. Mark the distances so you can place your feet behind the appropriate lines.

For more difficulty, perform the previous drill with this variation. Draw circles of about 8 centimeters (3 inches in diameter) on your partner's jacket with three different colors of chalk. Call the color that you will hit after you parry. This will help you shift your eyes to the target and see your point hit.

Allow your partner to call the color you are to hit. Make the circles on your partner's jacket smaller as you become more proficient. Put a number inside each circle, and you or your partner call the number or color you are to hit.

## Drill Variations

You or your partner can call the target area you will hit before the action begins, as partner thrusts, as you parry, or as you begin your riposte. You or your partner can call the designated target areas in response to the foot movements instead of the hand actions (as you retreat, as partner advances, before you advance, etc.).

Practice all the variations listed. Some of the selections will be very easy, and others will be more difficult for you to accomplish your goal. Fencing requires you to constantly expand your boundaries to improve and surpass your previous limits, emotionally and mentally, as well as physically. Most limitations are self-imposed and can be surpassed. Improve just 1 percent each day, and all perceived inadequacies and deficiencies are no longer obstacles—they melt away.

## SUCCESS SUMMARY

The parry and the riposte learned in this step create the balance needed for a fencer's game to be successful. As you master these moves you will begin to gain the self-confidence to handle whatever your opponent may throw at you. Remember the proper technique is important as is the distance and timing in order to be able to integrate the parry-riposte into your game.

Distance is a critical element you must consider with every action. The distance between you and your opponent influences and determines your accuracy. The correct blade work that is not accompanied with the appropriate footwork often has disappointing results.

You now have sufficient moves to work with others at your experience level. You will need to work on the actions learned in the first six steps for quite a while before you will feel comfortable with them in a competitive bout situation, but that will come in time. Actually, you will continue to strive to perfect these actions for as long as you fence. This is the miracle of fencing—the joy of striving for the elusive perfection.

# STEP 6

## FEINTS, DISENGAGES, AND BEATS: TAKING CHARGE

In this step you will learn offensive tactical moves to permit you to hit your opponent even though he is attempting to thwart that effort by parrying. Tactics are how you solve the bout. The actions you will learn are the feint, beat, and disengage.

Beats and disengages enable you to take charge of the opponent's blade or evade the opponent's attempt to take charge of your blade. The beat and disengage are similar to the engagement and the change of engagement. The beat is a spanking of the blade instead of just touching it, and the disengage avoids all contact with the blade during the movement from one side of your opponent's blade to the other. A feint is a bluff to mislead your opponent, causing him to try to take your blade, thereby allowing you the opportunity to avoid his blade and get the hit. The beats and deceptions are the fun part of fencing. You can have a level of control over your opponent that you never could have without these crafty moves.

## Why Are Feints, Disengages, and Beats Important?

Feints are used to help you learn how your opponent tends to react in certain situations. By simulating an actual attack, you often can learn what response your opponent likely will make and be a little better prepared for your opponent's reflex moves. Be careful not to get trapped into thinking that the action your opponent does in response to your feint will be the action he will perform when you attack. Remember, your opponent may also be very intelligent and realize the information he just gave you and deliberately change his response when you attack.

The disengage is helpful during your attack to avoid being parried. The disengage also can be used to prevent your riposte from being parried. It may be used to confuse your opponent. If your opponent cannot beat your blade it will be more difficult for him to hit you, take your blade, or put you in a compromising position, therefore giving you better control of the fencing bout. The disengage is important to avoid the opponent contacting your blade. It can also be used to frustrate your opponent in her attempt to set up something against you.

Beats can be used to disrupt your opponent's organization as part of a feint, or to distract him while you move in to hit or set up an action to score. The beat is used to remove the opponent's blade from interfering with your attack, thereby allowing you a clearer path to the target. Zbigniew Czajkowski, a well-known Polish coach and author, has made studies that show epee fencers are increasing the use of the beat on the blade as a preparation prior to the thrust and that the result is fewer double hits in epee. The beat helps to protect you from direct thrusts and other offensive measures by the opponent.

Circle beats (or counterbeats) are used to catch the opponent's weapon when she disengages your first attempt to beat, or they may be used to distract your opponent. These moves are very similar to the circleparries you learned in the prior step.

## How to Execute the Feint

The feint is similar to the thrust. The difference between the feint and the thrust is in the purpose and result desired. The feint is done at a particular time to get a response from your opponent and can be done from many distances. You feint to an area that the opponent is not protecting with his blade. You feint at a distance at which the opponent cannot hit you directly during your feint, however you create a situation in which the opponent feels he is in danger of being hit and responds accordingly (figure 6.1a and b). The purpose of the feint is to get a reaction from your opponent. The catch here is you cannot always know what the reaction will be, and you must be prepared for whatever reaction the opponent decides to make. Be prepared for surprises. Before you feint you have to know the reaction you would like to have and the responses the opponent could possibly make in the situation you have created. You must also know the response you are going to give in each of the feasible situations.

The most important element of this operation is that you have to be prepared to act on the response you get. Make no presumptions. You feint to procure information. Learn from your experience. You speculate but must never anticipate, and you need to see everything from its inception to its conclusion. The trick is not to mislead yourself. If you do not get a desired response from your opponent with one feint, change the timing or distance or footwork and try another feint. Do not fall in love with one particular feint and use it over and over again. Each feint needs to be slightly different. Remember, above all, that your opponent may choose not to respond as you would like. For a feint to be most useful, approach it as though you were offering your opponent a plate of cookies of varying kinds, allowing the opponent to make his choice, and then punish him by hitting him. Be prepared for the response or lack of response. Know your answer and be ready to respond correctly.

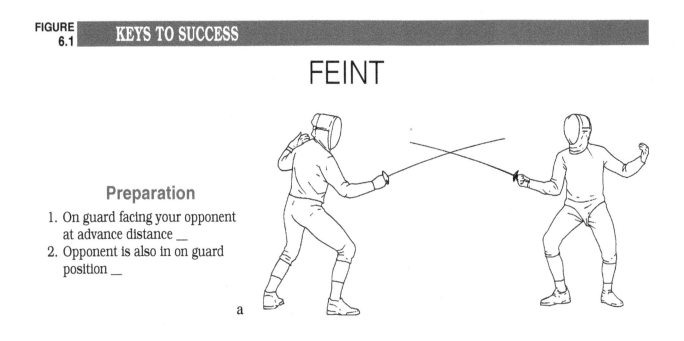

**FIGURE 6.1**  **KEYS TO SUCCESS**

# FEINT

### Preparation

1. On guard facing your opponent at advance distance __
2. Opponent is also in on guard position __

a

### Execution

1. Feint to her chest but stop when your point has just passed the opponent's bell __
2. Watch the reaction of the opponent __

### Follow-Up

1. Return arm to on guard position __

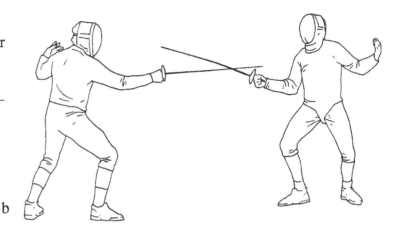

b

## SUCCESS STOPPERS

Do not be so crafty that your opponent doesn't see your feint. Don't be too arrogant or the opponent will score on you. Strangely enough, the most common mistake in making a feint is getting the anticipated reaction but not being prepared to respond. Another fault is a fencer's determination to force his opponent to respond in a particular way, thereby eliminating his ability to respond instinctively.

| Error | Correction |
|---|---|
| 1. Getting too close to opponent before feint. | 1. Make feint at a distance at which neither you nor your opponent can hit. |
| 2. Making an ineffective feint; holding it too long or too short. | 2. Feint must be clear without being forceful. Persisting too long makes the timing wrong. You must not attempt to force your opponent to reply. If you extend the invitation for too short a period the opponent does not have time to answer. |

## The Classic Disengage

We will discuss disengages using the under the blade technique (classic disengage) and retracting the blade technique (modern disengage) in this step.

## How to Execute the Disengage

The disengage is an evasive action taken to avoid the opponent's blade. You can go under, over, or retract your blade to avoid contact with the opponent's weapon. To do a classic disengage in the high line, you simply allow your tip to drop below the opponent's weapon, while she moves over the top of your blade attempting to parry 4 or 6, and reappear on the other side unscathed. The classic disengage requires your point to continue forward in a spiral movement during the disengage. You must not allow the point to retract but press it always forward. If the opponent is moving laterally, you only have to drop your tip directly underneath the blade and wait for the opponent's blade to pass over your point, and then you raise your point and thrust (figure 6.2a–d).

**FIGURE 6.2**    **KEYS TO SUCCESS**

# CLASSIC DISENGAGE

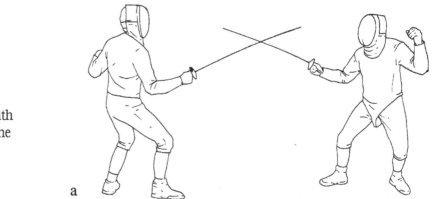

### Preparation

1. On guard facing opponent with your blade in outside high line (6) at advance distance __

a

b

## Execution

1. Make a short feint to opponent's chest__
2. Opponent does a parry 4 __
3. Drop your point below opponent's blade

   __
4. Opponent's blade passes over your point

   __
5. Raise your point on other side of opponent's blade, as your point continues to spiral forward __
6. Thrust to your target as you raise your point __

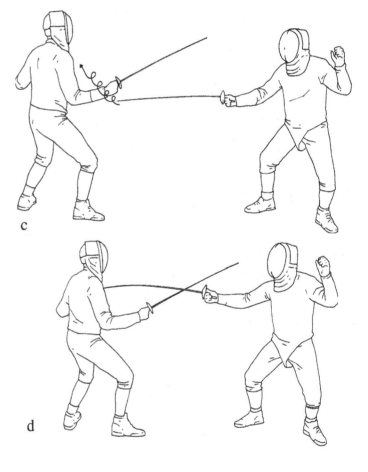

c

d

## Follow-Up

1. Return to on guard position __
2. Retreat out of distance __

The main problem of the classic disengage is moving independently of your opponent. It is critical that the classic disengage hit the opponent before or as he completes his parry.

| Error | Correction |
|---|---|
| 1. Making too large a movement with the point. | 1. Use your fingers to move the point in the smallest spiral possible. |
| 2. Pulling the arm back during the disengage. | 2. Press your point forward in a spiral movement. |
| 3. Beginning disengage too soon or too late. | 3. Observe the movement of opponent's blade with your peripheral vision and move your tip in sync with your opponent as she moves over your blade. |
| 4. Frantically trying to disengage all movement from opponent when there is nothing to disengage. | 4. Calmly move your blade using your fingers in rhythm with opponent's blade avoiding contact. |

# Modern Disengage for Foil Only

To execute a modern disengage you withdraw your point out of reach of the opponent's parrying plane and allow him to finish the lateral blade movement and then thrust to the target in the open area (figure 6.3). This disengage is to be used only in foil and not in epee. The advantage of the modern disengage is that you need to learn only one disengage for all the offensive and defensive blade movements. You don't have to move your point from the plane it is in; your point is always pointing directly ahead in a straight line from your elbow toward your target. This disengage must be used only when the opponent is moving his blade laterally, trying to contact your blade. Never withdraw your point when the opponent is thrusting. Remember that you only secure right of way when you begin making the thrust. The German Olympic Team has had great success using this form of disengage.

FIGURE
6.3

## KEYS TO SUCCESS

# MODERN DISENGAGE

### Preparation

1. On guard facing your opponent in lunge distance __
2. Blade is parallel to the floor pointed directly toward opponent __

a

b

### Execution

1. Feint __
2. Opponent begins parry movement __
3. Retract your point with your blade parallel to the floor still pointing at your opponent __

c

d

*(continued)*

### Follow-Up

1. When opponent's blade passes by your point, thrust your point forward to hit the opponent and lunge __
2. Return to on guard position __
3. Retreat out of distance __
4. Pause, hold your on guard position__

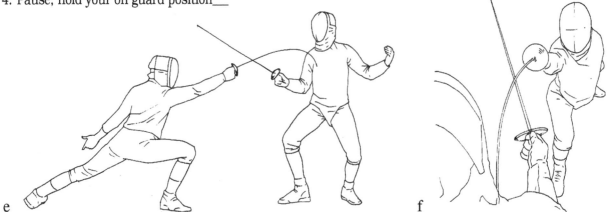

e                                                                    f

---

**SUCCESS STOPPERS**

It is important that you execute either the classic or the modern disengage as separate maneuvers. You cannot create a hybrid. A combination of the two disengages should not be done. It is critical that the opponent's blade is moving laterally, attempting to parry, and is not thrusting toward your target.

| Error | Correction |
|---|---|
| 1. Retracting point back too far or at the wrong time. | 1. Retract point only as far as necessary to evade the opponent's attempt to contact your blade. Elbow needs to stay in front of your body. Retract point only when opponent's blade is moving laterally and never when it is moving toward you. Keep your point always directed to the target and pressing forward. |
| 2. Not keeping blade parallel to floor. | 2. Keep blade parallel to floor and pointing toward opponent. Keep a straight line from your elbow to your point. Move point back and forth as if it were on a rail. |

## The Beat

When you practiced the engagement in a prior step, you contacted your opponent's blade lightly. For the beat, you contact the opponent's blade with a spanking movement. You create a crisp sound, a crack with a little more action in your blade, using your forearm and keeping your wrist firm.

## How to Execute the Beat 4

You can beat your opponent's blade only if your blade crosses his blade. Your tip starts toward your opponent's blade in a small arc followed immediately by hand and forearm, and then you snap your wrist and forearm, creating a sharp movement with your blade (figure 6.4a). Your blade stops suddenly on contact (figure 6.4b), transferring all your force to the opponent's blade.

Return your blade to its original on guard position with one slight alteration. Make your blade parallel to the floor. Do this for two reasons. First, the opponent may attempt to beat your blade back, and with your blade level it is more difficult for the opponent to contact your blade, and second, you need to position your blade for a quick, accurate hit.

**FIGURE 6.4**  **KEYS TO SUCCESS**

# BEAT 4

a

b

### Preparation

1. On guard in 6 position facing opponent __
2. Opponent is on guard also in 6 position__

### Execution

1. Move your tip first toward opponent's blade __
2. Snap your wrist __
3. Hold arm and wrist firmly when you beat__
4. Return to on guard position immediately after beat in one continuous movement without stopping __

### Follow-Up

1. Return to on guard position __

Fencers sometimes move their entire arm in the beat to try to have more force. However, a good beat comes from the forearm and fingers; a big arm movement notifies the opponent of your action and is much slower and easily seen. It is not uncommon to see a fencer move her blade away from her opponent's blade to try to get more force before beating. This is slower and can be easily disengaged.

| Error | Correction |
|---|---|
| 1. Allowing point to go beyond opponent's blade, pushing your opponent's blade. | 1. Contact opponent's blade with a crisp beat and return immediately to on guard. |
| 2. Moving elbow around. | 2. Anchor elbow—point elbow to the floor. |
| 3. Swinging your blade away from your opponent's blade before the beat to get more force. | 3. Move your point toward opponent's blade using your forearm and fingers. |
| 4. Trying to beat with your blade parallel to the opponent's blade. | 4. Make sure the blades cross at an adequate angle for the beat to be effective and not slide fruitlessly along the opponent's blade or miss completely. |

## Execution of Beat 6

Beat 6 is similar to the engagement in 6. Instead of touching the opponent's blade, spank it. Position your blade with the opponent's blade in your 6 line (on the outside of your blade). Move the tip of your blade first, followed immediately with a snap of the wrist and forearm to beat the blade. The wrist is held firmly. The forearm contracts forcefully. It is critical that the point begins to move first. Tip, hand, and forearm all finish together (figure 6.5). It is important to hear one sound; the blade should not slide.

FIGURE
6.5

**KEYS TO SUCCESS**

# BEAT 6

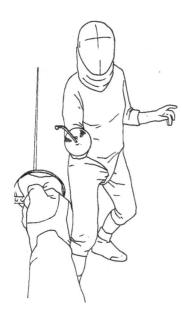

a

b

### Preparation

1. On guard facing partner __
2. Partner's blade is thrust at your shoulder __

### Execution

1. Move tip toward partner's blade first
2. Tip, wrist, and forearm arrive simultaneously in line to complete the beat __
3. Return arm to on guard position immediately __
4. Make the beat look and feel like one quick move __

### Follow-Up

1. Pause in on guard position__

## SUCCESS STOPPERS

Many fencers at this stage of their development get very excited and overreact to their opponent's blade, thereby swinging the blade in large movements, trying to hit opponent's blade. It is necessary to maintain a calm mental approach and execute the techniques with precision and accuracy. Use the beat as part of a plan; have a purpose for the beat. Do you want to get a reaction, or do you want to distract your opponent while you get closer. Use the beat frugally, making the beat more valuable. If you use the beat too often, it means nothing.

| Error | Correction |
|---|---|
| 1. Moving hand to 6 position without moving point first. | 1. Move tip, hands, and forearm as one, starting with tip. Lock wrist. |
| 2. Remaining on the blade after the beat. | 2. Move your blade from on guard to the beat and return to on guard as one quick movement. |

# DRILLS

All these drills and actions can be done on a partner, but go through the entire drill section first as it unfolds to be sure of your individual actions without the added variable of another fencer. Practice these drills each day on a target, as well as on a partner. Seek to be 1 percent better today than yesterday—technically, physically, mentally, and emotionally.

Position the back foot of your partner on a line, do not allow your partner to move her feet or lean into or away from your hit. It is easier to correct the distance if one of you is a constant, not moving.

Partner drills are more involved than you may first expect. The responsibility of the partner is tremendous. The drills outlined in this step minimize the action of the partner as much as possible. They focus on you executing an action, putting the responsibility on your shoulders. It is too easy for the partner to inadvertently cause difficulty before you perfect the actions. Be sure the partner is well padded. More padding is needed than in normal fencing because of the multiple hits received in one location. Hit the partner from the greatest distance you can and still have a firm hit.

For foil drills you may choose to use the classic or modern disengage in the drills. For epee, use the classic disengage.

## *1. Straight Feint Thrust*

On guard with your partner at advance distance. You thrust and your partner does not react; you then continue with an advance and hit your partner. Repeat this drill from lunge distance, using lunge to hit your partner instead of the advance.

 **Success Goal =** 10 consecutive times, hit your partner on the same spot with advance. Repeat 10 times with lunge ___

### ✔ **Success Check**
- Move point first ___
- Thrust definitively ___
- Look at the target ___
- Make corrections after each hit___

### **To Increase Difficulty**
- Draw three circles on opponent's chest, (as in diagram) with a number inside, partner calls which number you have to hit.
- Make advances and retreat before you start the action.
- Partner moves his blade around, but does not touch your blade or block your hit.

### *To Decrease Difficulty*
- Perform drill slowly.

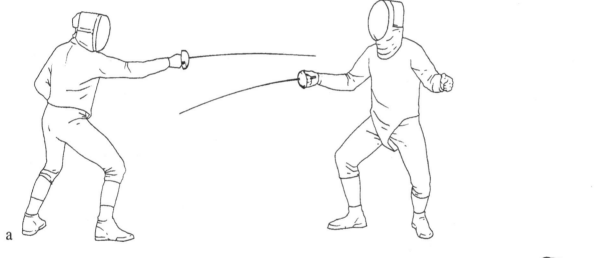

a

b

## 2. Feint, Beat 4, Hit

On guard with your partner at advance distance. Your partner's blade is in pointed at your knee. You feint and your partner moves his blade to on guard position; you then beat 4, thrust and hit your partner with an advance. Repeat this drill from lunge distance, using lunge to hit your partner instead of an advance.

**Success Goal** = 10 consecutive actions, making a crisp beat 4 on your partner's blade with advance and with lunge ___

**Success Check**
• Move tip first to beat___
• Lock your wrist as you beat ___

**To Increase Difficulty**
• Increase repetition to 20 without stopping.
• Partner changes distance requiring you to select the correct footwork for the distance.

**To Decrease Difficulty**
• Make the movement slowly.
• Break movement into its component parts.
• Partner tells you when to start each action.

## 3. Feint, Disengage 4, Hit

On guard with your partner at advance distance. You feint and disengage your partner's parry 4; continuing thrust, you advance and hit your partner. Repeat this drill from lunge distance.

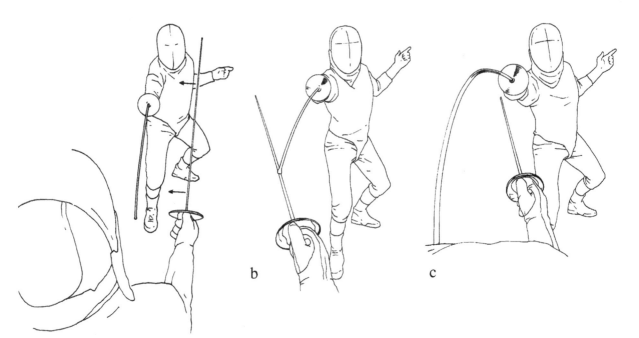

a                b                c

**Success Goal** = Do not allow your partner to contact your blade when you disengage his parry 4. Repeat 10 times with advance and 10 times with lunge ___

**Success Check**
- Keep disengage as small as possible, using fingers ___
- Complete disengage before you start footwork ___
- Make your disengage spiral forward if using classic disengage ___
- Make your disengage in response to your partner's parry, not too early and not too late ___

**To Increase Difficulty**
- Advance with your first thrust, your partner retreats, continue with the action.
- Make advances and retreats before you begin the drill.
- Partner makes small, quick parries.
- Partner tries to contact your blade in 4 at different times during your feint.

**To Decrease Difficulty**
- Partner makes slow parry movement.

## 4. Feint, Disengage 6, Hit

On guard with your partner at advance distance. You feint and disengage your partner's blade as he does a circle 6 parry; you thrust and hit your partner with an advance. Repeat this drill from lunge distance.

**Success Goal** = Do not allow your partner to contact your blade when you disengage his circle 6 parry. Hit the partner in the same spot each time. Repeat 10 consecutive times with advance and with lunge ___

**Success Check**
- Begin your disengage as your partner begins his circle 6 parry ___
- Keep your point as close as possible to partner's blade ___
- Make the disengage and hit in one continuous movement ___

**To Increase Difficulty**
- Partner alternates between lunge and advance distance.
- Partner continuously changes distance.
- Partner takes 6 at different moments during your feint, he varies the timing.

**To Decrease Difficulty**
- Partner tells you when to do each action.
- Partner takes a slow 6.
- Break the action into separate parts.

### 5. Beat 4, Hit

On guard with your partner at advance distance. You beat 4, your partner responds by beating your blade in 4, you beat again in 4, thrust with advance and hit your partner. Repeat with lunge.

**Success Goal =** 10 consecutive times, respond immediately with your beat 4 when your partner beats your blade. Repeat with advance and with lunge ___

#### ✔ Success Check

- Focus on the timing of your partner's reaction, beat his blade quickly after he touches your blade, but do not beat into his beat ___
- Beat with the point of the blade, keeping the bell in the same place ___
- Do not allow partner's beat to move your blade more than 10 to 15 cm before you respond ___
- Complete your bladework and thrust before you move your feet ___

#### To Increase Difficulty

- Partner changes rhythm of his beat each time.
- Partner advances and retreats before the action.

#### To Decrease Difficulty

- Stop after each beat.
- After your beat, your partner waits before beating your blade.

a

b

c

d

### 6. Beat 4, Disengage 4, Hit

On guard with your partner at advance distance. You beat your partner's blade in 4. You then disengage his attempt to beat your blade in 4, thrust, and hit with lunge. Action is the same for epee and foil.

**Success Goal =** 10 consecutive times, make your action one continuous movement, hitting your partner on the same spot each time ___

**Success Check**

- Focus on the timing and reaction of your opponent ___
- Do not stay on partner's blade ___
- After you beat, place your blade in thrusting position (blade flat) to help you have a smooth disengage___
- Use small blade movement, spiraling the blade forward ___

### 7. Feint, Disengage, Beat 6, Hit

On guard with your partner at advance distance. Your partner feints and disengages your parry 4, you then beat 6, thrust, and hit your partner with lunge.

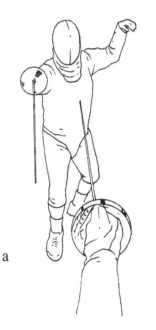

a

b

*(continued)*

c

d

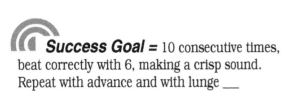**Success Goal =** 10 consecutive times, beat correctly with 6, making a crisp sound. Repeat with advance and with lunge ___

### ✔ Success Check

- Use your fingers and wrist to spank the blade ___
- Move forearm as little as possible ___
- At the moment you beat, thrust to your partner___
- Lock your wrist as you beat ___

### To Increase Difficulty
- You and your partner use continuous footwork.

### To Decrease Difficulty
- Partner stops after each part of the action.
- Partner keeps point higher.
- Perform action slowly.

### 8. Feint, Disengage, Beat 4, Hit

On guard with your partner at advance distance. Your partner feints and disengages as you do a circle 6, you then beat 4, thrust, advance, and hit your partner. Repeat with lunge.

**Success Goal =** 10 consecutive times, make the drill one continuous action, with a crisp beat 4, and hit your partner in the same spot each time. Repeat 10 times with lunge ___

**Success Check**
• Visualize each activity before you begin ___
• Beat 4 using only the point ___
• Thrust definitively after beat ___

**To Increase Difficulty**
• Partner makes disengage very small.
• Partner varies the speed of his action.
• Partner changes the distance.
• Hit the same spot on your partner.

**To Decrease Difficulty**
• Pause after each move.
• Partner makes slow movements.

## SUCCESS SUMMARY

The disengage is important to evade your opponent's attempts to capture your blade while you are in the process of making an attack. The beat is used to remove the opponent's blade from interfering with your attack, thereby allowing you a clearer path to the target. The circle beats are used to catch the opponent's weapon when they disengage or beat your blade. The feints are used to invite your opponent to respond before you complete your attack, thereby permitting your opponent to commit to a course of action before you do.

All of the actions taught in this step add the variability to make fencing the physical chess game that it is. You hit because you can get your opponent to protect one region while you attack another. This is done in much the same way that a good broken-field runner in football can cause a tackler to miss completely. In both fencing and football, it is not the sheer speed or power, it's being where they aren't.

# STEP 7

## PARRY-RIPOSTE LOW LINE: DEFENDING AGAINST THE STEALTH ATTACKS

The low-line parries are parry 2, parry 7, and parry 8. Your blade action deflects the blade of the attacker away from its intended destination, your target area. You also can defend yourself by moving out of distance or by counter attacking. In epee you thrust to hit the nearest available target. In foil you thrust to target area and must prevent your opponent from hitting you even after you hit. You should not use counterattack in foil very often. The parry, in the low line as in the high line, can be taken when you retreat, stand still, or even when you advance.

Defending and riposting from the low line is a little more perplexing than defending your upper body. To defend the low line areas you must focus and think of the opponent's weapon as a real threat and defend your thigh just as you would your face. The reflexes must be learned and trained repeatedly until they are automatic reflexes. The riposte must be just as much a reflex as defending your face.

The low-line parries are done in response to an offensive maneuver by the opponent. In foil the right of way is important. By definition, the attacking action is a beat, and the defending action is called a parry. You must riposte immediately in order to score the touch. You must feel the compelling desire to score. Do not parry just to defend yourself—parry with the inten-

tion of scoring a touch. Parry and riposte aggressively.

## Why Is the Low-Line Parry-Riposte Important?

The low-line parry-riposte is extremely important for you to become a well-rounded, successful fencer. If you work the high line, only the lower half of your body is an unguarded target area. If you do not defend the lower area adequately the opponent soon will discover this weakness and exploit it. You must fence with no fear. You want to limit the options of the opponent as much as possible, and the low-line parry-ripostes and counter attacks are an excellent way to decrease the attacks available to the opponent.

The counter attack in epee when opponent is attacking the low line is a great way to steal touches. The top of the hand, the head, and shoulders are exposed and unprotected.

For foil fencers the opponent will attack under the elbow, to the flank, or rib area, hoping you will not see the attack until it is too late to parry. For epee fencers you can look for attacks to the thigh or foot. Never limit your focus or concentration to one area. Always be prepared to parry-riposte any attack.

## How to Execute a Parry in the Low Line

The parry in the low line, like that for the high line, is a defensive maneuver. There are a number of accepted variations on the parries and ripostes in the high line; the low line has even more. A good moment to use the low-line parries, like the high-line parries, is the moment the attack begins or during the last phase of the attack, just when the opponent thinks the attack will arrive.

For foil the low-line area of your target is farther away from the opponent than that of the high line, giving you slightly more time to react. For epee the low-line target areas (toe and thigh) are closer to your opponent. Keep in mind that the degree of extension of your weapon arm during the parry will depend on the distance you are from your opponent when you parry. Reach forward to parry the attacking blade the moment you perceive an attack, or wait until the very end of the opponent's attack, just before it lands. The epee fencer should parry or counter attack anything made toward the foot or knee immediately because the distance between these target areas and the opponent is closer than the upper body.

## How to Execute the Parry 7

The parry 7 is similar to the parry 4, in that they both protect the inside line, but for parry 7 the point is below the bell guard. The parry 7 is used to deflect the blade of the opponent when the attacking blade is directed to your inside low line. Parry 7 is not used very often to defend in epee. The parry is made by moving the blade clockwise (for right hand) from the on guard position across the body with the tip of the weapon lower than the bell. The tip moves first, followed immediately with hand and forearm, all reaching the parry position together. The blade moves in a small dynamic arc toward your opponent's blade. The arm extends slightly, reaching for the attacking blade. The wrist may change position slightly (depending on the distance at which you are parrying) but must be held firmly to control your blade and have a deflecting effect on the opponent's blade. After contacting your opponent's blade, move your blade quickly, pointing directly toward target. A straight line is formed from the tip to the elbow, prepared for the next action—the riposte. The elbow stays directed toward the floor (see figure 7.1). This position prepares you to hit the target accurately and consistently. If you stay on the opponent's blade as you hit, the action is called opposition parry.

**FIGURE 7.1**

## KEYS TO SUCCESS

# PARRY 7

### Preparation

1. On guard in 6 position facing opponent in 8 position ___
2. Move weapon in clockwise (for right hand) arc diagonally toward opponent's blade ___
3. Keep wrist slightly bent to allow tip to be lower than bell and slightly to the left as you contact ___

### Execution

1. Move tip first, then hand and forearm ___
2. Keep elbow pointed at floor ___
3. Move weapon laterally across your body in a sweeping arc ___
4. Extend arm slightly as you parry ___
5. Point is directed to the thigh of the opponent ___

### Riposte for Foil

1. Perform a beat parry ___
2. Bring blade to thrusting position ___
3. Keep blade and forearm parallel to floor ___
4. Riposte to target and hit ___
5. Return to on guard ___

### Riposte for Epee

1. Hold parry position after completing the parry ___
2. Stay on opponent's blade ___
3. Riposte to the target and hit the thigh with the bell guard slightly higher than the point ___
4. Return to on guard ___

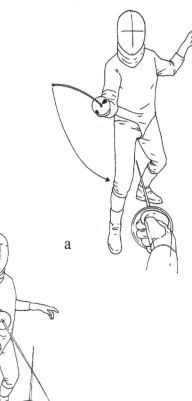

a

b

c

d

One success stopper is positioning your hand, arm, and shoulder in a weak and ineffective position. Remember to move the 7 in a small arc that contacts the opponent's blade like the parry 4, except the point is lower than the bell guard with your palm turned slightly up and thumb at 1 o'clock position.

| Error | Correction |
|---|---|
| 1. Making the movement of weapon and arm too wide. | 1. Snap blade with fingers and wrist and move point and bell a small amount. |
| 2. Holding handle or grip too loosely. | 2. Hold your grip tightly and keep your wrist firm so you can control your point and your opponent's blade. |
| 3. Raising bell too high and dropping point too low. | 3. Hold blade in strong position; point is directed to target. |

# How to Execute Parry 8

The parry 8 is called a low-line outside parry like the parry 6 for the high line. Parry 8 is similar to the parry 6, except the bell and forearm are lower, and the tip of the weapon is lower than the bell. From the on guard position the tip, bell, and forearm move in an arc counterclockwise down and out to contact the opponent's blade (figure 7.2).

This parry is a movement of the blade to defend against an attack directed to the forward flank or rib area in foil, or to the flank, hip, thigh, knee, shin, or foot in epee. The parry is made by moving the blade in an arc from 6 position toward the outside of your hip. The tip of the weapon finishes below the bell and is the first to move, followed immediately by the hand and forearm, all strongly reaching the parry position together. The wrist is held firmly, and the forearm muscles contract forcefully and stop abruptly in a straight line just outside your thigh.

The epee fencer uses this parry often and will need a stronger parry with a slightly more extended arm than the foil fencer. Epee fencers must contact the opponent's blade with the intent of not allowing the opponent's point to hit, even after the parry. The defending epee fencer has to hit the opponent before the attacker can hit him, thus the need for stronger contact with the opponent's weapon. The epee or foil fencer may stay on the opponent's blade to riposte. This is called an oppositional parry. If you beat the blade and do not maintain contact, it is a beat parry.

FIGURE 7.2  **KEYS TO SUCCESS**

# PARRY 8

### Preparation

1. On guard position in 6 position___
2. Opponent thrusts to your flank for foil and to your thigh for epee ___

### Execution

1. Move tip first, then hand and forearm, finishing together with thumb up ___
2. Keep elbow pointed at floor ___
3. Move parry in an arc counterclockwise for right-handed (clockwise for left-handed) over top of partner's blade___
4. Extend slightly as you parry ___
5. Finish the parry with point directed toward the opponent's thigh___
6. Direct point to target. Riposte (in foil, aim for the abdomen or flank; in epee, to the chest, hip area, or lower)___

### Follow-Up

1. Foil: immediately return to on guard position after riposte ___
2. Epee: keep arm extended while you return to on guard position after riposte ___

a

b

c

d

Most errors in parrying are due to incorrect technique, wrong distance, and misjudging timing. If you try to parry at the wrong distance you cannot control the opponent's blade.

| Error | Correction |
|---|---|
| 1. Making movement too large. | 1. Move bell slightly outward, finishing a small arc using the fingers and forearm. The wrist is held firmly to create a straight line to the point from the elbow. |
| 2. Dropping the bell too low. | 2. Keep elbow pointed to the floor. Bell should stop about waist high and your thumb should be at 1 o'clock position. |
| 3. Using the wrist too much. | 3. Keep wrist firm. |

# How to Execute Parry 2

The parry 2 is similar to the parry 8 except you turn your hand over, thumb inside at 9 o'clock position. It is used to defend the same area as the parry 8 (low outside), except it is much stronger. The parry 2 defends against an attack to the rib area in foil, or to the rib, flank, hip, thigh, knee, shin, or foot in epee. An advantage to using the second parry is that it can also be used to protect a larger area.

From the 6 position, the parry 2 is made by turning the palm down and moving the blade laterally in a counterclockwise arc toward the outside of your hip. The tip of the weapon should finish below the bell and is the first thing to move, followed immediately by the hand and forearm, all strongly reaching the parry position together. In foil, the wrist should be cocked slightly up and held firmly on contact with the attacking blade. The arm does not extend fully with the parry 2 (figure 7.3).

From the on guard position the hand rotates palm down as the move progresses. The tip, bell, and forearm move in an arc down and out to encounter the opponent's blade, finishing with the palm toward the floor and contacting the opponent's blade on the little-finger side of the blade. This parry is the most powerful parry in the low line and is used frequently in both foil and epee. The parry 2 is even more powerful if you step in to riposte after you make the parry instead of extending your arm fully. Allow your point to move horizontally, past your thigh. Bring the point back in line just as you extend the arm slightly and hit. Opponent's blade should be held on your bell as you make the riposte.

The epee fencer will vary the position of the point depending on the target the opponent is attacking. To defend the foot, the tip should be pointed more downward; to defend the knee and thigh, the point should be higher, and to defend the hip and flank area, it should be in the same position as in foil. Epee fencers must contact the opponent's blade with the intent of not allowing the opponent's point to hit, even after the parry, by keeping contact with the opponent's blade.

**FIGURE 7.3**  KEYS TO SUCCESS

# PARRY 2

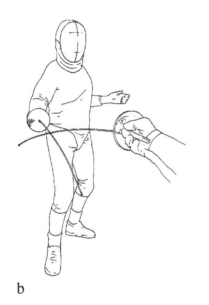

a                                      b                                      c

### Preparation

1. On guard with weapon in 6 position ___
2. Opponent on guard with weapon pointing toward your hip___

### Execution Phase

1. Move tip first, then hand and forearm, all finishing together ___
2. Move blade in a small, counterclockwise arc___
3. Rotate hand, finishing the move with the palm down ___
4. Keep bell level or slightly lower than elbow ___

### Follow-Up

1. Return blade to on guard position ___

## SUCCESS STOPPERS

A main problem is raising the elbow and allowing it to move around, thereby making the movement very large. Move the point in a small circular motion.

| Error | Correction |
|---|---|
| 1. Raising the bell and elbow in preparation to parry. | 1. Keep your elbow steady, moving it as little as possible. Use your forearm, not your wrist. |
| 2. Parrying down into your thigh instead making the parry finish outside the limits of your body. | 2. Move your arm in an arc instead of directed toward your thigh. Focus on hand and arm stopping just outside thigh. |
| 3.Making exaggerated wrist movement. | 3. Stop your point just past your opponent's thigh. Use your fingers to disengage. |

## How to Execute the Riposte From the Low-Line Parries by Classic Disengage

You use a disengage after you parry when your opponent tries to parry your riposte. After you parry, begin the extension to the target. Be prepared to disengage but do not anticipate a parry by your opponent. Looking for a parry will make you slow down. This slowdown will allow your opponent to parry your riposte

The riposte by disengage depends solely on the action of the opponent. A classic disengage done in response to a low-line parry must be done over the top of the blade. The first requirement is that you recognize which parry the opponent is attempting. After you discern this, just lift your point over the top of the opponent's blade. The direction will be obvious as you see his blade moving toward yours. As soon as the opponent has passed your point, thrust to the target. You must not allow the point to retract in the classic disengage but always press it spiraling forward, using the fingers (figure 7.4).

**FIGURE 7.4**

**KEYS TO SUCCESS**

# RIPOSTE FROM LOW LINE
# BY CLASSIC DISENGAGE

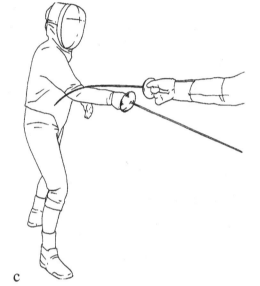

a          b          c

### Preparation

1. On guard facing opponent in advance distance ___
2. Opponent attacks you in the low line ___

### Execution

1. You parry 2, 7, or 8 ___
2. Direct your point to target in low line ___
3. Make a small movement forward with your point ___
4. Opponent attempts to parry 2, 7, or 8 ___
5. Lift your point to allow opponent to pass under your blade ___
6. Drop your point on the other side of opponent's blade, thrust, advance, and hit___

### Follow-Up

1. Return to on guard position after riposte and retreat to correct distance ___

The critical part of the riposte is the timing and distance. Riposting from too far away, too late, or too early will prevent you from scoring. You may need to hold the parry until you are in good distance to riposte with extension, advance lunge, or fleche, which you will learn in step 9. The disengage must be done at the moment the opponent attempts to parry your blade and not before.

| Error | Correction |
|---|---|
| 1. Not making a timely riposte. | 1. You must thrust to riposte. If opponent parries, then you disengage. Don't hesitate to riposte. |
| 2. Making disengage too large. | 2. Keep your blade as close as possible to opponent's blade or bell guard. |

## Circle Parries

Knowledge of the circle parries in the low line is important so you can parry your opponent's blade in the event he disengages your first attempt to parry. If the opponent attacks you, disengages your lateral parry, and continues in the same line, a circle parry may be called for.

## How to Execute a Circle Parry 2, 7, or 8

The low-line circle parries are basically the same as the circle parries of the high line. The opponent makes a low-line feint and disengages your move to parry. The circle parry requires you to turn your lateral parry into a circle by moving the tip of your weapon in a circle over the top of your opponent's blade. Chase your opponent's blade, contacting it as he makes his thrust to hit. You maintain the same hand position as in the lateral parry for 7 and 8 (figure 7.5). For the 2 parry, turn your palm down.

# CIRCULAR PARRY 2, 7, OR 8

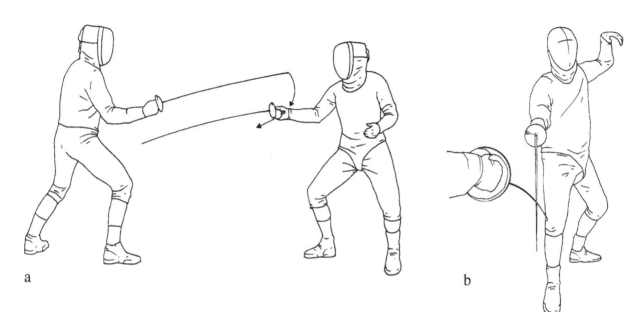

a

b

### Preparation

1. On guard in 6 position facing opponent ___
2. Your partner makes a low-line attack to one of these lines: 7 or 8 (2 and 8 are in the same line, just different hand positions for the parry) ___

### Execution

1. Move to parry position and you do not catch the opponent's blade ___
2. Opponent disengages your parry ___
3. Follow opponent's blade around lifting your tip over top of opponent's blade ___
4. Spank the opponent's blade and stop your blade abruptly on contact___

### Follow-Up

1. Return to on guard with blade in thrusting position___
2. Be ready to make hit ___

## SUCCESS STOPPERS

Ignoring the low-line attacks or not recognizing them as attacks for even a fraction of a second is the cause of many unnecessary hits. Indecision is catastrophic. Successful decisions are the result of experience. Experience grows from a huge number of bad decisions. Decide and act. Action is educational. Don't become paralyzed and don't hesitate. Look for what you can learn from each situation and act on it.

| Error | Correction |
| --- | --- |
| 1. Making first parry too large. | 1. Tighten forearm forcefully and lock your wrist to stop lateral movement in correct parry position. |
| 2. Making circle too large, using wrist. | 2. Follow opponent's bell guard with your tip making a tight circle. |
| 3. Raising elbow to the side. | 3. Raising the elbow can be a result of weakness in the arm and shoulder, or tension in the shoulder and neck. Strengthen the hand, arm, and shoulder girdle. Press down with the shoulder and point elbow toward the floor. |

**PARRY-RIPOSTE LOW LINE**

# DRILLS

### *1. Parry 7*

This drill will help you learn to defend your low line target against attacks. On guard facing opponent in 6 at advance distance. Partner advances and thrusts to your low inside. You parry 7 and thrust to touch opponent. For epee you may hit the hip or below. For foil and epee you may parry and make a straight riposte to chest.

**Success Goal =**

Parry opponent's blade so that you do not accidentally get hit. Riposte to same target area 10 times___

**Success Check**

- Move point first from 6 position in an arc down to the left ___
- Move bell and forearm slightly to the inside ___
- Extend your blade slightly as you parry opponent's blade ___
- After you parry, direct the point of your blade to the area you intend to touch ___

**To Increase Difficulty**

- Keep contact with the blade and hit.
- Do drill from lunge distance.
- Add advances and retreats. Your partner leads, he stops, and thrusts to target.
- Riposte to different target areas.

**To Decrease Difficulty**

- Do drill very slowly.
- Stop after each component of the drill.

## 2. Circle Parry 7

On guard facing partner at advance distance. Partner feints to your low line and advances as you retreat and attempt to parry 7. Partner lifts her blade over the top of your blade just as you attempt to parry and continues to your low line. You follow partner's blade around in a circle parry, contacting partner's blade as she completes the disengage. You then riposte to opponent's flank or chest; for epee you may also aim for hip and thigh.

### Success Goal =
Parry correctly and touch opponent in designated spot 7 of 10 attempts ___

### Success Check
• Move point first ___
• Reach forward for partner's blade; do not pull your arm back ___
• Contact blade firmly ___
• Do not allow your blade to swing wildly ___

### To Increase Difficulty
• Opponent changes distance for riposte and you must choose correct footwork.
• Riposte to low line (thigh for epee).
• Stay on opponent's blade and riposte. Your partner must not try to block you from making the riposte.

### To Decrease Difficulty
• Do all blade work from extension distance.
• Return to on guard; do not riposte.

## 3. Parry 8 With Riposte

On guard facing opponent at advance distance. Your partner thrusts to your hip area under your bell. You parry 8 and riposte with advance to hit low-line target (flank for foil).
For epee, thrust to the thigh or flank, staying on your opponent's blade (closing parry).

### Success Goal =
Parry correctly. Riposte in designated spot 7 of 10 attempts ___

### Success Check
• Move point first ___
• Opponent's blade should be near your bell ___
• Stay on opponent's blade for epee; for foil you may stay on partner's blade or beat-parry and riposte to another line ___

### To Increase Difficulty
• Partner beats your blade before he thrusts.
• Opponent changes distance for riposte. You must select appropriate footwork.
• For foil and epee beat-parry 8 and riposte to different target area.

### To Decrease Difficulty
• Break the action down into components.
• Do the action slowly.
• Parry, hold parry and do not riposte. Return to on guard.

## 4. Beat Parry 8 With Disengage

On guard facing partner in 6 at advance distance. Partner thrusts to your hip area and advances, you beat, parry 8 and retreat, feint to partner's chest. Partner attempts a parry 6. You disengage, advance, and riposte to chest. For foil, use modern or classic disengage. For epee, use classic disengage.

### Success Goal =
Touch opponent in designated spot 7 of 10 attempts ___

### Success Check
- Hold wrist firmly ___
- Move point in small arc to parry and disengage ___
- Keep elbow down ___
- Move point first for riposte ___

### To Increase Difficulty
- Increase speed.
- Opponent calls for different places for riposte.
- Advance and retreat before partner thrusts.
- Partner beats your blade before he thrusts.
- Opponent changes distance for riposte; you select appropriate footwork.

### To Decrease Difficulty
- Do the action slowly.
- Break action down into its components.

## 5. Circle Parry 8 Riposte

On guard facing partner in 6 at advance distance. Partner feints to your flank for foil or hip area for epee with an advance. You retreat and take a parry 8. Partner disengages over the top of your blade, advances, and continues the attack to the low line as you retreat and follow opponent's blade around, completing your circle parry 8. Stay on partner's blade and riposte with advance to flank. For epee you may riposte to thigh as an alternative.

### Success Goal =
Parry and hit accurately 8 of 10 attempts ___

### Success Check
- Retreat in on guard position ___
- Keep wrist firm___
- Move point in small arc ___
- Keep elbow down, line should be straight from the point to elbow___
- Hold opponent's blade on your bell in strong 8 position as you hit___

### To Increase Difficulty
- Start action from different footwork.
- Riposte with lunge.

### To Decrease Difficulty
- Perform drill slowly.
- Stop after each component of the drill.

## 6. Parry 2 Riposte

On guard facing partner in 6 at advance distance. Partner thrusts to your flank or hip area and advances. You retreat and do a parry 2 and riposte with advance.

### Success Goal =
Parry correctly and riposte accurately 8 of 10 attempts to designated area ___

### Success Check
- Move point first___
- Move your point in a small arc ___
- Rotate hand to palm down as you move to parry ___
- Do not extend your arm to parry___
- Do not raise shoulder ___

### To Increase Difficulty
- For epee do parry 2 and riposte to a different area each time. First riposte is to the hip, second riposte is to the thigh, and third is to the foot. Repeat sequence. For foil, riposte to flank, holding blade. Then riposte to chest without opponent's blade.

### To Decrease Difficulty
- Do drill slowly.
- Stop after each part of the action.
- Hold parry and return to on guard. Do not riposte.

## 7. Parry 2 With Disengage

Start on guard facing partner at advance distance. Partner feints to your low line and advances, you retreat and parry 2. Then feint to partner's chest; your partner parries 6 and you disengage and hit chest with advance. Feint and hit are made from thumb up position.

### Success Goal =
Touch opponent in designated spot 8 of 10 attempts ___

### Success Check
- Move point first___
- Be sure bell and blade are outside your hip line when you parry___
- Move point in small arc ___
- Feint definitively___
- Disengage with your fingers___
- Hold wrist firmly___
- Rotate hand to thumb up position as you thrust___

### To Increase Difficulty
- Advance and retreat before partner thrusts ___
- Partner beats your blade before he thrusts ___
- When you parry 2, press partner's blade before your release to thrust___

### To Decrease Difficulty
- Do the action slowly ___
- Break action into component parts ___

## 8. Controlled Bouting

Begin on guard with an opponent. Use the entire strip—move aggressively forward and backward. Your partner will make a real attack to your low line. You are to parry the attack with a parry 2 and riposte where you like. If you choose to riposte to your partner's chest, your partner may try to parry 6 so you can practice your disengage. Partner does not parry if you riposte to lowline.

### Success Goal =

Bout one minute, rest one minute. Score a minimum of one hit during each bout of one minute.

### Success Check

• Maintain good on guard position___

### To Increase Difficulty

• Move in and out of distance faster.
• Opponent makes more attacks.
• Recover to on guard immediately after each attack and start the next action where you are. Do not return to on guard lines.
• Bounce continuously.

### To Decrease Difficulty

• Opponent tells you when she will attack.
• Perform the actions slowly.
• Opponent waits for you to parry and allows the riposte.

## SUCCESS SUMMARY

The critical part of the low-line parries is the position of the bell when you riposte—particularly with the closing parries. When you stay on the blade, you must hold your blade firmly and your bell must be outside your body line to be effective. Complete entire action using the best technique you can. Correct and improve 1 percent each time you practice. World and Olympic champions train, drill, take lessons, fence, and strive to improve every day.

# STEP 8

# LOW-LINE OFFENSIVE MOVES: VARIETY ADDS SPICE TO YOUR GAME

In this step we will explore the offensive blade movements of the thrust, feint, engagement, change of engagement, beats, and disengages in the low line. The low line is the area below your bell when you are in on guard position. The target area in foil is the lower torso, and in epee it also includes everything below the hips.

From an on guard position, engagement in the low line is done by the crossing of blades with the points being lower than the bells. The low-line change of engagement requires you to go over the top of the opponent's blade instead of below it. The same is true for the disengage. As in the high line, the change of engagement in the low line is an excellent preparation for offensive and defensive actions. The beats directly evolve from the engagement and change of engagement. You can use the beats in a variety of ways. You can use hard beats to knock the opponent's blade away from the target area it is defending, or you can use light beats to manipulate your opponent and get information. Each will receive distinctly different reactions from your opponent.

## Why Are Low-Line Actions Important?

The offensive maneuvers in the low line are necessary to enhance and vary your game. They enable you to alter your game, to adapt to your opponent, and to exploit his weaknesses. Low-line attacks are harder for the opponent to see than attacks to the high line. Mastering your diversity and conquering your opponent will assist you in becoming a well-rounded fencer.

The engagement and the change of engagement are important in order to collect more information about the opponent and to help you develop command of the blade. The change of engagement, beat, and disengage in the low line are used to confuse, control, and deceive your opponent.

The low-line moves reveal another half of the body to score on. They help support your goal of maintaining pressure on the opponent, not allowing him to relax and compose a plot against you. The off-balanced and bothered opponent is easier to distract while you manipulate and guide him into compromising situations so you can score. The low-line actions make a well-rounded foil fencer. For epee, it is essential to have good low-line skills.

The straight thrust to the low line can be very successful because, in foil particularly, most thrusts are made to the chest. It is akin to the "end around" in football. It adds variety to the offensive game, and when used at the right time, it can surprise the opponent. A thrust below the opponent's elbow works well for many reasons. One, you can hide your blade under the opponent's hand; your tip is not visible to your opponent. Two, the opponent's parries are usually not as well developed in the low line as they are in the high line, especially in foil. Three, the opponent is usually surprised. And four, a hit in the opponent's flank (the side) is a wonderful building block for other actions, including the feint. Keeping your opponent unsure of your next move is a perfect way to keep her off balance, mentally as well as physically.

For epee a straight touch to the thigh is an excellent change of pace and forces your opponent to defend a much larger target area. In addition, the thigh is relatively easy to hit. Fragmenting your opponent's concentration and ability to focus on defending limited target areas is also a goal of the low-line actions.

## How to Execute a Low-Line Thrust

The low-line thrust is done in a manner similar to the thrusts in the high-line, with the difference being the target area toward which you are pointing. A low-line thrust is a thrust made below the opponent's bell when he is on guard (figure 8.1). For foil it is the flank or rib area; for epee it also includes the legs. The thrust is made by a smooth, quick extension aimed directly at the area you intend to hit. For you to hit directly with the thrust, the opponent must have no warning signs of your coming move. You must not tighten the shoulder or make any unnecessary body movements.

## How to Execute the Feint

The feint is the same as the low-line thrust, but you do not intend to hit with the first action. To be successful your opponent must believe the actual intent of the feint is to hit and thereby respond by attempting to defend themselves. If you are too subtle, the feint may lose its effectiveness. The low-line feints must be done with different tempos, varied distances, and various preliminary actions to induce the opponent to become entangled in your conspiracy (figure 8.2). A feint should be an invitation for the opponent to accept. The opponent must respond as he would to an attack. You must not persist too long with the feint or the opponent can take your blade, counterattack or take other defensive or evasive measures.

**FIGURE 8.1**

**KEYS TO SUCCESS**

# LOW-LINE THRUST

### Preparation

1. On guard in 6 position, lunge distance from your partner___
2. Focus on the target and relax shoulder ___

### Execution

1. Hold blade firmly with the fingers ___
2. Smoothly thrust to low-line target, hitting target___
3. Do not lock your elbow___

### Follow-Up

1. Return to on guard position ___
2. Do a quick self-analysis ___
3. Select one segment to improve ___

**FIGURE 8.2**

**KEYS TO SUCCESS**

# LOW-LINE FEINT

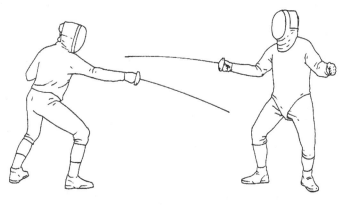

### Preparation

1. On guard in 6 position at lunge distance___
2. Focus on the target you are to hit ___

### Execution

1. Thrust but stop short of the hit ___
2. Maintain balance ___
3. Don't overcommit ___
4. Allow your training partner or opponent the opportunity to respond; don't try to make her respond to your feints; be smooth ___

### Follow-Up

1. Return to on guard position ___
2. Do a quick self-analysis ___
3. Absorb one element of the action that was correct ___
4. Select one segment to improve ___

**SUCCESS STOPPERS**

The failure to have a straight line between shoulder and point will diminish your distance and cause thrusts to fall short and feints to be unheeded. You must reach fully for the target area. The greatest and most common problem with making a successful feint is demanding your opponent respond to your feint as you want him to, thereby staying too long in the feint.

| Error | Correction |
|---|---|
| 1. Being unprepared for your opponent's response. | 1. Be alert. |
| 2. Locking the elbow and raising the shoulder. | 2. Keep elbow loose and shoulder down. |
| 3. Moving legs before the feint. | 3. Bend knees and move front foot one inch as you feint. |

## How to Execute a Low-Line Engagement and Change of Engagement (Change the Line)

Get on guard in low-line position facing your opponent. The tips of your weapons should be lower than your bells. Position yourself at a distance where you can engage (touch) your opponent's blade with your arm about three-quarters extended (figure 8.3). The training partner's blade remains stationary, and you move your blade from one side of the partner's blade to the other. Change sides by moving your tip over the partner's blade using your fingers. Make the smallest movement possible. Touch the opponent's blade on each side; stop at each contact of the blades.

**FIGURE 8.3**

**KEYS TO SUCCESS**

# LOW-LINE ENGAGEMENT AND CHANGE OF ENGAGEMENT

### Preparation

1. On guard in low line facing opponent in advance distance ___
2. Keep tips lower than the bells ___
3. Weapon arm is three-quarters extended ___

### Execution: Engagement

1. Touch opponent's blade firmly on one side ___
2. Return to on guard ___
3. Touch opponent's blade firmly on the other side ___

### Execution: Change of Engagement

1. Engage training partner's blade on one side ___
2. Move your blade over top of opponent's blade ___
3. Make movement small, easy, and effortless, using only fingers ___
4. Engage opponent's blade on the other side without returning to on guard___
5. Engage firmly___

### Follow-Up

1. Return to on guard in 6 position ___

## SUCCESS STOPPERS

Some people are distracted by the opponent touching their blade. Practicing engagements will help you become more confident with blade contact and also help you learn to control the opponent's blade.

| Error | Correction |
|---|---|
| 1. Contacting the training partner's blade too harshly and moving too quickly from side to side. | 1. Touch the blade smoothly with your blade. |
| 2. Having floppy wrist, thereby making blade movement too large and uncontrolled. | 2. Move your tip over the top of opponent's blade using a small blade movement with the fingers, keeping wrist firm. |
| 3. Touching the blade too close to the bell. | 3. You need to touch the opponent's blade. You will not have control or the ability to feel the opponent's blade if you touch the blade close to the bell. Your exploration is best served by touching the opponent's blade firmly but gently. |

## The Low-line Beats

The low-line beats 7, 2, and 8 are basically the same as parry 7, 2, and 8 except you contact the blade with a crisp beat and do not maintain contact with the blade. Refer to step 7, low-line parries for beat 7, 2, and 8.

## How to Beat 7

The 7 covers the lower inside quadrant while the 4 covers the high inside quadrant (figure 8.4). Touch the opponent's blade underneath. Contact the blade similarly to the 4, but the difference is that you and your opponent are both in the low line. Your opponent's blade is in your low inside line. Keep wrist firm, beat lightly; it is not a strong move in itself but can be very effective to befuddle your opponent. Move your tip first, followed with the bell and forearm reaching the end position together. Snap the blade just a little on contact to create a sharp spanking movement. Blade moves in a semicircular clockwise arc downward to contact a blade that is directed straight at you with point below waist level. Beat 7 is made with your point being lower than your bell.

FIGURE
8.4

**KEYS TO SUCCESS**

# BEAT 7

### Preparation

1. On guard at advance distance in 6___
2. Partner thrusts to your inside low line___

### Execution

1. You move your blade toward your partner's blade in a semicircle movement clockwise and downward from on guard position___
2. Keep wrist firm___
3. Tip points toward opponent's upper thigh as beat is finished___
4. Stop the blade on contact___

### Follow-Up

1. Return blade to on guard position___
2. Do not stay on blade ___

## Beat 8

The beat 8 is a most useful beat in the low outside line. Your tip is below your bell. Beat the opponent's blade firmly, keeping your wrist straight. Your thumb remains at the 1 o'clock position. From the on guard position move your blade down in a counterclockwise arc. Your blade contacts the opponent's blade with your point directed to your opponent's thigh.

## How to Perform a Beat 2 (Seconde)

The seconde protects the same area as 8. The 2 is a much stronger move than the 8 and can be used in a variety of ways that the 8 cannot. From on guard position, drop tip down in a semicircle and rotate your hand to palm-down position,

thumb finishing at 9 o'clock. Your blade stops outside your hip line about hip high. Your point is directed toward opponent's hip. The difference between this beat and all the other beats you have learned is the rotation of the hand and forearm.

### How and When to Disengage

Disengages depend on the reflexes and moves of your opponent. You must not predetermine to disengage but be prepared for the possibility. If you beat the opponent's blade and the opponent's response is a return beat, you have created a situation to disengage. A direct feint to the low line also may stimulate your opponent to defend herself by making a parry 7, 8, or 2, thereby creating a situation for you to disengage and hit. The disengage in the low line to a parry 7, 8, or 2 is done by lifting the point of your weapon up and over the opponent's blade as he performs his lateral movement.

## LOW-LINE OFFENSIVE MOVES

# DRILLS

For epee, the low-line hits for the drills below may be to any target area below the hips. Generally, the hits are to the broader hip area, the thigh, or the toe. For foil the hits are to the rib or flank area.

### 1. Hit Them Below the Belt

Low-line feint, disengage, and hit.

On guard in 6 position, facing partner at lunge distance. Feint to partner's hip; partner makes a slow parry 8. You disengage partner's parry and lunge to hit. In foil hit your partner in the flank. Do not allow the training partner to touch your weapon, but if he contacts your blade, continue smoothly with the disengage during this drill. The goal is to prevent him from contacting your blade, but in the beginning contact may occur until you develop the timing and feeling of the disengage.

In epee the thigh is the target and is closer to you than the rest of your partner's body. Your point should avoid the parry in the same way as in foil. In epee if the training partner happens to touch your blade during the disengage, you continue by slipping around the training partner's weapon and continuing with your action to hit as you would during a bouting situation. The right-of-way rule does not exist in epee, so you do not lose right-of-way when the partner touches your blade as you do in foil.

**Success Goal =** Hit training partner on designated target 10 of 15 attempts ___

**Success Check**
• Hold point steady ___
• Make disengage as small as possible ___

**To Increase Difficulty**
• Disengage during your lunge.
• Perform action with advance lunge, disengaging as your partner parries at different moments during your attack.

**To Decrease Difficulty**
• Complete disengage and thrust before the feet move.
• Partner takes a large parry 8.
• Do the action slowly.

## 2. Circle 2 Hit

On guard in 6 facing your partner in 8 position at advance distance. Engage your partner in 7, you then do a circle 2 beat, then raise point, thrust, and hit in chest by lunging as partner retreats.

**Success Goal =** Hit training partner in designated area 10 of 15 attempts ___

**Success Check**
- Rotate your hand with thumb stopping at 9 o'clock position___
- Beat training partner's blade briskly with dry sound___
- Thrust with thumb up ___

**To Increase Difficulty**
- Hit training partner in flank for foil; for epee, hit training partner in thigh.

**To Decrease Difficulty**
- Hit with advance, partner remains still.

a

b

c

d

### 3. Beat 7, Hit

On guard in 6 facing your partner at lunge distance. Your partner's blade is in 8 position. Beat partner's blade in 7, thrust, lunge, and hit partner in chest.

**Success Goal =** Hit training partner in designated area 10 of 15 attempts ___

**Success Check**

- Move tip first to beat your partner's blade in 7 ___
- Move tip first to hit target ___
- Arm is three-quarters extended in foil before lunge. Arm is fully extended for epee but not stiff and locked ___
- Accelerate the last six inches of the attack ___

**To Increase Difficulty**

- Add mobility before action.
- For epee, hit partner's thigh or arm.
- Do the drill with advance lunge.

**To Decrease Difficulty**

- Do the drill with advance instead of lunge.

### 4. Circle Beat 7

On guard at lunge distance, engage partner in 8 position. You do a circle beat 7. Feint with an advance to partner's chest, your partner retreats and circle parries 6, you disengage and thrust with a lunge to hit partner in chest (partner retreats only once).

**Success Goal =** Hit partner in designated area 10 of 15 attempts ___

**Success Check**

- Move tip first using fingers___
- Feint with a definitive thrust ___
- Make small disengage___

**To Increase Difficulty**

- Your partner sometimes varies his response when you feint. He does not always parry. You must continue your feint into a thrust and hit in one continuous action when he does not parry.

**To Decrease Difficulty**

- Perform action slowly. Stop after each movement.
- Perform drill on verbal command from your partner.

### 5. Circle Beat 8 With Disengage, Hit

On guard, engage partner's blade in 7 position, advance distance from your partner. Your partner pushes back on your blade in 7 as you perform a circle beat 8 then feint to chest. Partner parries 6 and you disengage and hit partner in flank or chest for foil; for epee hit the flank, chest, or thigh.

**Success Goal =** Hit partner in designated area 10 of 15 attempts ___

**✔ Success Check**

- Form a straight line from the tip of your weapon to your elbow as you engage in 7; do not extend your arm fully ___
- Make your beat 8 with a firm wrist and forearm ___

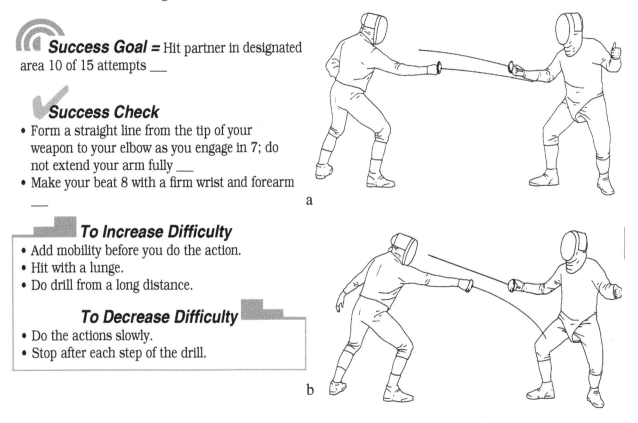

a

b

**To Increase Difficulty**

- Add mobility before you do the action.
- Hit with a lunge.
- Do drill from a long distance.

**To Decrease Difficulty**

- Do the actions slowly.
- Stop after each step of the drill.

### 6. Defender's Choice

On guard with your partner at lunge distance. Engage in 6. You feint to partner's flank for foil or hip area for epee as you make an advance. Partner slowly makes a parry 8 or 7 with retreat. Your partner will alternate between the 7 and 8 parries. She will allow you time to disengage. After you disengage, thrust, lunge, and hit. Partner does not retreat. Choose a different target to hit for each action.

**Success Goal =** Hit partner in designated area 10 of 15 attempts ___

**✔ Success Check**

- Disengage before you lunge ___
- Make disengage with fingers small and precise ___

**To Increase Difficulty**

- Use mobility before action begins
- Partner speeds up parry and does not wait for you.
- Partner varies the time he chooses to parry your feint.

**To Decrease Difficulty**

- Pause after each component.
- Partner tells you which parry he will take before he parries.

### 7. Engage and Change Engagement in 8 and 7

On guard at lunge distance engage partner in 8. You and your partner change engagement twice. On the next exchange you disengage the partner's change of engagement and do not allow training partner to touch your blade. You extend, lunge, and hit partner in low line before partner finishes the change of engagement. Your partner must not retreat out of your distance. For next action engage partner's blade in 7; repeat drill.

**Success Goal** = Hit partner in designated area 10 of 15 attempts ___

**Success Check**
- Make change of engagement smoothly ___
- Allow partner to contact your blade after each change of engagement until you disengage and hit ___

**To Increase Difficulty**
- Add mobility, changing direction as you change engagements.
- Vary the number of times you change engagement before you disengage and hit.

**To Decrease Difficulty**
- Pause after each change of engagement.
- Partner changes engagement slowly and allows you to disengage and hit.

### SUCCESS SUMMARY

Your goal in using the low-line offensive moves is to add variety to your game and to require your opponent to use all of his defensive tools. You also want to keep him unsure of your next move. By probing all of his defensive actions, you are more likely to find unguarded area, which you can then attack. With a wide variety of actions at your disposal, you are more likely to surprise your opponent with your actions. The larger the target, the more chances you have to score. You also force your opponent to make more errors.

# STEP 9

# LONG-DISTANCE FOOTWORK: CONQUERING VAST SPACE

You already have learned the advance, retreat, lunge, and bounce. In this step we will introduce two types of fleche. The most popular classic fleche is a type of footwork that covers long distance with great speed; the second type of fleche is taught to beginners and is used as a preparatory exercise to the classic fleche. We will call this second type a crossover fleche, to easily distinguish it from the classic fleche.

The fleche is a running step used to extend your range. The fleche enables you to reach your opponent at a longer distance than can be reached by the lunge. The fleche is a flying movement, an airborne attack. Its success depends on the timing and distance from which you begin the fleche. Speed and surprise also play a part. Different from the lunge, the fleche calls for the rear foot to be brought forward past the front foot. The fleche can be preceded by an advance or bounce to gain an even longer distance or by a retreat to draw your opponent forward and then change direction with great speed. The fleche should appear sharply from nowhere and stun the opponent.

To execute the fleche, your weapon arm first extends toward the target. This is key to a great fleche; you should have a feeling that the point of your weapon is pulling your body forward in a straight line. If you fleche quickly you will be unable to stop when the hit occurs. Fleche directly at your opponent, and immediately after the hit occurs, run by your opponent quickly, passing her on the unarmed side. Never practice the fleche on a stationary target such as a wall, where you cannot run past the target. Make each action correct in coordination and timing. Most important, be sure your body position is correct.

The crossover fleche uses similar foot movement as the classic fleche, but the body behaves more as it does in the lunge. You recover to on guard position in front of the opponent. It is an option that allows you to cover a longer distance than the lunge and keep one foot on the ground, which makes it easier for the novice fencer to begin learning the technique of the fleche. The charm of this action is that it is so simple to do and can be used in conjunction with the lunge to lure the opponent to fence with you at a slightly closer distance. Several lunges that land short of the opponent can capture his attention and allow the opponent to measure the distance from which you can hit. Then you can do a crossover fleche or classic fleche and reach the unsuspecting opponent.

## Why the Fleche Is Important

The fleche enables you to hurdle a great stretch of distance in a short period of time. It allows you to hit your opponent when the distance is great and when he is off balance and not prepared to defend himself. The crossover fleche permits you to cover more distance than the lunge without being airborne as you are in the classic fleche; it does not require the full commitment to the attack as the classic fleche.

### Tactical Use of the Fleche

The fleche is used very often by shorter fencers because they cannot reach the opponent using a lunge. The fleche can be done using a variety of footwork. It can be done after an advance, a bounce, a retreat, a lunge, etc., but the best time is when your opponent is moving forward. The fleche allows you to attack with power, efficiency, and effectiveness.

The rear foot is brought forward past the front foot in a running type of movement. You should touch your opponent just before the rear foot lands. When executing the fleche you must not contact the opponent with your body but continue to run past her without touching her. If there is body contact between the fencers it is called corps a corps, which is forbidden. A warning is given to the fencer causing the corps a corps.

## How to Execute the Fleche

The execution of the fleche from the on guard position is done by extending your arm and then commanding a powerful driving force with both legs, launching your entire being forward like a shot, propelling yourself toward the opponent airborne and soaring, transcending gravity, and culminating in a hit (figure 9.1). Everything in your mind and body is committed to this mercurial action. This extravagant move, wild and reckless, poses an avenue that is difficult to defend. Continue the fleche and run past the opponent. The opponent can hit you after you pass, but you cannot hit your opponent after you have run past him. Your best defense is to run quickly past your opponent. To make the fleche after the advance is easier, and you can cover a longer distance.

# FLECHE FROM AN ADVANCE

### Preparation

1. On guard facing your partner at advance lunge distance __

### Execution

1. Begin extending the weapon arm __
2. Advance __
3. Thrust and then push with rear leg __
4. Extend rear arm and push with front leg __
5. Hit opponent before rear foot lands on the floor __
6. Keep body in profile __

### Follow-Up

1. After the hit, continue to run past your opponent without touching him with your body __
2. Pass on unarmed side of your opponent __

a

b

The fleche must be done from the correct distance. This is when the hit can occur before your rear foot lands on the floor. It is very important that the fencer start the fleche by extending the arm before the legs move so she will have time to react correctly to the response of the opponent.

| Errors | Corrections |
|---|---|
| 1. Starting with the legs before extending the weapon arm. | 1. Extend your weapon arm three-quarters of full extension before you begin the leg movement of the fleche. |
| 2. Not pushing with front leg. | 2. Extend arm fully and push powerfully with the front leg. |
| 3. Keeping legs too straight. | 3. Bend legs and stay in low position. |
| 4. Running into one's opponent. | 4. Remember to go around your opponent. |
| 5. Going "up" instead of "forward." | 5. Push with legs after you have lost your balance leaning forward. |

## How to Fleche From Retreating

It is very important when you retreat before the fleche to put the front foot on the floor and create more pressure on the front leg before you begin the fleche (the front leg is the power for your fleche, figure 9.2)

Be sure to smoothly shift your center of gravity. The rear foot pushes strongly and rapidly, toes pointing forward in same direction as the front foot in a running movement. The rear foot should step forward before the opponent has completed his advance, before he is able to change direction and begin retreating. Keep your front hip forward as your feet retreat; do not shift weight back. Change direction subtly and suddenly, extending your arm fully. Hit your opponent in the shoulder area before your rear foot lands on the floor.

**FIGURE 9.2**  **KEYS TO SUCCESS**

# FLECHE FROM A RETREAT

### Preparation

1. On guard position facing your opponent at lunge distance___

### Execution

1. Opponent advances ___
2. You retreat as opponent advances
3. Extend weapon arm ___
4. Push front hip forward ___
6. Push with rear foot and step forward bringing knee up high ___
7. Push strong with front foot ___
8. Keep body fully stretched out as you hit opponent before your rear foot lands on the floor ___

### Follow-Up

1. Accelerate as you run past your opponent on his unarmed side without stopping___
2. Keep your trunk turned sideways until you pass your opponent ___

---

**SUCCESS STOPPERS**

Tension in the shoulders and neck cause problems with the fleche, preventing you from extending your arm before the head, body, or legs begin to move forward. Keep knees bent and weight equally balanced on your legs, with slightly more on the front.

| Error | Correction |
|---|---|
| 1. Starting with the legs. | 1. Extend weapon arm before you push with the legs. |
| 2. Straightening the legs and raising your rear hip up. | 2. Keep your legs bent and your chin up as you fleche. |
| 3. Shifting the weight back over the rear foot. | 3. Keep weight equally distributed before your start your fleche. |
| 4. Starting the fleche too late when the opponent is retreating. | 4. Start the fleche as the opponent begins the advance. |
| 5. Turning rear shoulder forward. | 5. Press rear shoulder back, extend rear arm, and stay sideways. |

## How to Execute the Crossover Fleche

The crossover fleche for beginners is very deceptive because it has an exceedingly long range. The crossover fleche is a move that brings the rear foot forward into a long step (figure 9.3). So the length of your attack is determined from the position of your front foot, not the back, concealing the distance your attack will cover. Extend your weapon arm and push hard with the rear leg. Drive hard with the front foot. The rear foot lands on the heel forward of the front foot. You must keep your shoulders in one line and in profile position. You must hit your opponent before your rear foot lands. Do not allow the body to drop down or slump forward. This is an upright move with the chest out. Recover forward or backward into an on guard position.

The rear shoulder must not turn past the front shoulder in foil. The rules of foil do not allow this change of position without penalty. If your rear shoulder comes forward you do not get the touch, and your opponent can be awarded a point. Extend the rear arm backward as you do in the lunge to prevent this from happening. In epee there is no requirement for the shoulder placement.

FIGURE
9.3

**KEYS TO SUCCESS**

# CROSSOVER FLECHE

### Preparation

1. On guard position facing opponent in fleche distance ___

### Execution

1. Extend weapon arm ___
2. Push with rear leg and step forward ___
3. Push with front leg hard ___
4. Keep your head up and chin level ___
5. Keep shoulders level ___
6. Rear leg lands on heel ___

### Follow-Up

1. Follow through with front foot in the forward position again ___
2. Pivot rear foot into on guard position, toes pointing to the side ___

a

b

## SUCCESS STOPPERS

The crossover fleche will be effective only if you can maintain control and remain in balance.

Always intend to hit, but be prepared for surprises.

| Error | Correction |
|---|---|
| 1. Dropping the head down. | 1. Keep the head up and the chin level. |
| 2. Moving the body before the weapon arm extends. | 2. Extend your arm before your legs, head, or body move. |
| 3. Moving body up and down. | 3. Keep shoulders in the same line and stay in profile position. |

## LONG-DISTANCE FOOTWORK

# DRILLS

### 1. Fleche

You may fleche using the classic or crossover fleche. On guard with your partner at fleche distance. You extend and fleche. Your partner may need to retreat just after you hit to make the situation more realistic, yet still safe.

**Success Goal** = Hit your partner 10 consecutive times in the same spot on the shoulder
___

**Success Check**
• Extend arm first, pressing point forward ___
• Push with legs ___
• Keep head up ___
• Keep your eyes on your target and be sure to keep your eyes open ___
• Run past your partner after the hit ___
• Do not touch your partner with your body ___

**To Increase Difficulty**
• Make two advances and three retreats, stop, and then fleche; partner keeps distance.
• Bounce in same place, then fleche.

**To Decrease Difficulty**
• Do the fleche slowly.

## 2. Advance Fleche

On guard facing your partner in fleche distance. Your partner retreats, you advance, and when your partner stops, you fleche. Hit on target and run by your partner 10 consecutive times.

**Success Goal =** Fleche when your partner stops retreating ___

**Success Check**

- Start arm first ___
- Do not fleche while partner is retreating ___
- Advance the same distance your partner retreats ___

**To Increase Difficulty**

- Draw two circles (with numbers or colors inside the circle) on partner's chest.
- Partner calls the number you are to hit as you begin your fleche.
- Bounce in same place , then advance fleche.
- Advance, squat, touch floor, then fleche.

**To Decrease Difficulty**

- Do the fleche slowly.

## 3. Retreat Fleche

On guard in fleche distance. Your partner advances and you retreat. Your partner stops and you fleche from your retreat.

a

b

c

**Success Goal =** Hit partner 10 consecutive times in same spot without missing the target ___

### ✔ Success Check

- Extend arm, pressing point forward ___
- Keep body in profile ___
- Keep weight equally distributed on both feet, shifting center of gravity forward ___
- Be sure to put your front foot on the floor, completing the retreat, before you begin your fleche ___

### ◢ To Increase Difficulty

- Partner makes two advances, you keep distance, and then you fleche.
- Partner varies between two advances and one advance before stopping.

### To Decrease Difficulty ◤

- Make action slowly.

## 4. Disengage Fleche

On guard at advance fleche distance. Your partner makes a small advance and moves her blade into parry 4 position. You fleche as she starts to advance and disengage her 4. You *must* extend your arm first before the feet move to be able to disengage.

**Success Goal =** Hit partner 5 out of 10 fleches without allowing your partner to touch your blade.

### ✔ Success Check

- Extend arm fully and disengage before feet move ___
- Be sure the distance is not too close for you to fleche safely ___

### ◢ To Increase Difficulty

- You advance and retreat, your partner keeps distance.
- You make continuous retreats. Stop retreating and fleche on partner's advance as he parries 4.

### To Decrease Difficulty ◤

- Partner does not advance. You start from fleche distance.
- Perform the action slowly.

## 5. Option Fleche

On guard with partner in fleche distance. Your partner makes two retreats and two advances using the same size steps. You follow, and when you feel the moment is correct, you execute the fleche.

**Success Goal =** 10 consecutive times, you keep correct distance and fleche at the correct moment hitting designated target___

**Success Check**
- Maintain good on guard position ___
- Keep knees bent ___
- Stay focused on relaxing shoulder and moving point first with fingers ___

**To Increase Difficulty**
- Partner increases speed of footwork.
- Partner changes rhythm of footwork.
- Partner changes pattern of footwork and step size.

**To Decrease Difficulty**
- Stop after each advance and retreat.
- Do the drill slowly.

## 6. Quick Fleche

On guard with your partner in fleche distance. Your partner's blade is in 8 position. You fleche to your partner's shoulder when you choose, and your partner tries to parry your blade with 6 parry before you can hit the target. Your partner cannot lean back or retreat.

**Success Goal =** Hit your partner 2 out of 10 fleches ___

**Success Check**
- Stay relaxed ___
- Make action smoothly and quickly and start moving the point without tensing the shoulder ___
- Keep your eyes open and watch the point hit the target ___
- Keep head up ___

**To Increase Difficulty**
- Partner alternates between parry 4 and parry 6.
- You stand still and your partner advances and retreats; you choose the time to fleche.
- Partner stands still and you advance and retreat. Be sure you fleche from the correct distance.

**To Decrease Difficulty**
- Fleche from shorter distance.
- Partner parries slowly and allows you to hit.

### 7. Decision Fleche

You are on guard with your partner at fleche distance. You lead the footwork by making three advances and two retreats. You feint and your partner chooses to make parry 4 or parry 6. You only fleche and disengage when your partner does a parry 6, not when he does a parry 4. If your partner does a parry 4, you retreat out of distance quickly.

Do the same drill, but fleche when your partner does a parry 4, and retreat out of distance when he does a parry 6.

**Success Goal =**

• Hit your partner 5 out of 10 tries making the correct decision by fleching only when partner does parry 6 __

• Repeat drill and fleche only when partner does a parry 4. Choose correctly 5 out of 10 times

__

**Success Check**

• Feint aggressively without being overly committed. Make your partner feel he must respond __

• Retreat quickly when the parry is not the one on which you are to fleche __

• Make decision to fleche or retreat quickly __

**To Increase Difficulty**

• Your partner leads the footwork. You choose the right time to feint.

• You bounce instead of using steps to advance and retreat.

**To Decrease Difficulty**

• Do the actions slowly.

• Partner tells you on which action to fleche when you are doing the footwork.

### 8. Mobile Fleche

On guard with your partner in fleche distance. You lead the footwork by doing three advances and two retreats; your partner follows. Your partner thrusts, you parry 4 or parry 6 and riposte with fleche.

#### Success Goal =

Perform correctly 8 of 10 consecutive actions, hitting partner in same spot on shoulder. You must parry and thrust before your body moves for the fleche ___

#### Success Check

- Fleche from low on guard position ___
- Footwork must be at a speed your partner can follow ___
- Parry partner's blade and thrust before beginning fleche ___

#### To Increase Difficulty

- Have partner only respond once for every three feints.
- Parry 4 with five fleches and parry 6 with five fleches.
- Allow partner to decide line of attack—4 or 6.

#### To Decrease Difficulty

- Advance and retreat slowly.

## SUCCESS SUMMARY

The success of the fleche depends on your timing, distance, and technique. You must try to hit your opponent before your rear foot lands on the floor. You must maneuver your opponent into a position where you can hit before he has time to retreat out of distance. Capture him the moment he is not prepared for your fleche. You will begin to feel and understand the timing and distance from which to fleche during the drills and then incorporate these into your bouting. The more drills you do, the faster you will learn the technique, timing, and distance.

# Rating Your Progress

Rate your progress by writing the appropriate number in the space to the right of each skill. Add the numbers when you finish and check the key that follows to get an indication of your progress.

**5** = Excellent    **4** = Above average    **3** = Average    **2** = Below average    **1** = Unsuccessful

1. On guard _____
2. Advance _____
3. Retreat _____
4. Bounce forward _____
5. Bounce back _____
6. Holding the french grip _____
7. Holding the pistol grip _____
8. Target practice _____
9. Mobility chancing direction _____
10. Extension _____
11. Lunge _____
12. Recovery forward from lunge _____
13. Recovery backward from lunge _____
14. Straight thrust _____
15. Engagement (Low-line, High-line) _____
16. Change of engagement (Low-line, High-line) _____
17. Parry 4 _____
18. Parry 6 _____
19. Riposte _____
20. Circle parry 4 _____
21. Circle parry 6 _____
22. Feint _____
23. Classic disengage _____
24. Modern disengage _____
25. Beat 4 _____
26. Beat 6 _____
27. Parry 2 _____
28. Parry 8 _____
29. Parry 7 _____
30. Riposte from low-line _____
31. Riposte by disengage _____
32. Riposte by classic disengage _____
33. Riposte by modern disengage _____
34. Circle parry 2 _____
35. Circle parry8 _____
36. Circle parry 7 _____
37. Classic Fleche _____
38. Cross over fleche _____
39. Low-line feint _____
40. Low-line thrust _____
41. Beat 2 _____
42. Beat 8 _____
43. Beat 7 _____
44. Cycle beat 2 _____
45. Circle beat 8 _____
46. Circle beat 7 _____
47. Success of attacks _____
48. Success of defense _____
49. Understanding offense _____
50. Understanding defense _____

51. Understanding bouting \_\_\_\_
52. Ability to alternate between offense and defense \_\_\_\_
53. Limiting destructive self-talk \_\_\_\_
54. Ability to focus during the bout \_\_\_\_
55. Persistence \_\_\_\_

56. Ability to come from behind \_\_\_\_
57. Planning and understand bout tactics \_\_\_\_
58. Flexibility, ability to change tactics in the middle of a bout \_\_\_\_
59. Ability to learn from watching your opponent \_\_\_\_
60. Goal setting \_\_\_\_

Total \_\_\_\_

| Score | Progress |
|---|---|
| 100-110 | Excellent |
| 90-100 | Above average |
| 80-90 | Average |
| Less than 80 | Below average |

You can use these ratings for each skill as a method to assess which steps you need to work on the most. This is particularly useful for helping you plan which drills to concentrate on.

Even when your rating reaches the "Excellent" level, don't think that your work is done. There's always room for improvement!

# GLOSSARY

**Absence of blade** – when fencing blades are our of engagement, the blades are not in contact with each other

**Advance** – a type of fencing mobility, a step forward from an on-guard position

**Advance distance** – the distance from which you can hit your opponent by making a forward movement of the blade by extending your sword arm towards your opponent and making an advance

**Aggressively Defensive** – pressing your opponent aggressively while waiting for the opponent to make a move so you can hit him with his own action.

**Attack** - an offensive movement designed to score a hit against an opponent.

**Balance** - controlling your body. The ability to maintain equilibrium and remain steady, light and controlled on your feet while moving freely backward and forward.

**Beat** – crisply contacting the opponent's blade with your blade with a spanking action

**Beat 2** – contacting your opponent's blade with your blade when your opponent's blade is in your low outside line

**Beat 4** – contacting your opponent's blade with your blade when your opponent's blade is in your high inside line

**Beat 6** – contacting your opponent's blade with your blade when your opponent's blade is in your high outside line

**Beat 7** – contacting your opponent's blade with your blade when your opponent's blade is in your low inside line

**Beat parry** – a defensive action that deflects the attacker's blade done by crisply contacting the blade of the attacking opponent with your blade

**Bell guard** - the rounded metal plate shaped shield in front of the handle that covers and protects the hand. It is also used to protect the body.

**Blade** – long slender flexible steel, extended part of the weapon, used to deliver hits on the opponent. It is also used defensively to protect your target.

**Bounce** - a type of fencing mobility. A slight spring done, in the on-guard position, by the feet and arches with a minimum amount of movement in the knees, used to move forward and backward

**Bout** - a competition between two fencers. A match between two fencers in which hits are counted to a specific number and a winner is determined.

**Change of engagement** – changing the contact with the opponent's blade from one line or side to another, touching it lightly but firmly. Engaging the opponents blade in a new line.

**Change-the-line** – the movement of the blade from one fencing line to another

**Circle beats** – an offensive move done by moving your blade in a small circle to contact the opponent's blade. You contact opponent's blade crisply with a spanking beat. Often you move from one side of the opponent's blade to the other, (if opponent disengages you will contact the blade on the same side)

**Circle parries** – a defensive move done by moving your blade in a small circle to contact the attacting opponent's blade firmly.

**Circle parry 4** – a defensive move used when the opponent is attacking to your high inside line, chest area. It is done by moving your blade in a small counterclockwise circle to contact the attacking opponent's blade.

**Circle parry 6** – a defensive move used to protect against attacks to your high outside line (sword arm and shoulder area). It is done be moving your blade in a small clockwise circle to contact the attacking opponent's blade.

**Classic disengage** – an evasive action done to avoid an opponent's attempt to contact your blade. It is done by dropping the tip of your weapon below opponent's weapon, as he attempts to contact your blade, your blade continues to spiral forward toward opponent's target area.

**Classic fleche** - footwork that covers long distance with great speed. An attack make by a running type maneuver propelling you into a flying action forward.

**Corps a Corps** – When two fencers are touching so then they cannot move their weapons efficiently.

**Crossover fleche** – a forward type of foot-work that covers a longer distance than the lunge. An attack made with a running type foot-work motion that brings the rear foot forward of the front foot into a long step. You do not fly.

**Counter attack** – an attack or thrust to the nearest unprotected target of the opponent during an opponent's attack

**Counter-parry** – a circular parry

**Danger zone** – the distance between two fencers where touches can be scored. The distance between you and your opponent at which you can be scored on, as well as score on your opponent.

**Defense** – Protecting yourself by using foot-work and blade-work.

**Direct attack** – an attack made straight to the target without diversion.

**Direct riposte** – riposte made straight to the target

**Disarm** – dropping or loosening one's grip on his weapon

**Disengage** – evading an opponents attempt to contact your blade.

**Dominant foot** – strongest foot usually the front foot when in on-guard position

**Engagement** - the touching and maintaining light but firm contact with the opponent's blade

**Engagement in the low line** - the crossing of blades with the points being lower than the bell guards

**Epee** – The dueling sword. It has a large circular bell guard and flexible triangular blade. Fencers may hit and score anywhere on the opponent's body, both fencers may score at the same time. There is no right-of-way.

**Extension** – moving the point of your weapon forward toward the target by straightening your weapon arm.

**Extension distance** - the distance between a fencer and his target which requires solely the extension of the arm to hit the designated target with the point of the weapon.

**False attack** – an offensive movement (fake attack) or trick which is not intended to score a hit but the purpose being to make the opponent believe it is an attack with the intent of scoring

**Feint** - a bluff to mislead your opponent. An offensive movement made to resemble an attack in order to draw a reaction from the opponent.

**Fencing strip** – The described area on which fencing takes place, long and narrow, 16 meters by 2 meters.

**Fleche** – a type of fencing mobility, a running kind of step used to extend your range to score on your opponent.

**Foil** – a fencing weapon with a small bell guard and rectangular flexible blade. It was originally designed as a practice weapon for epee. There are right-of-way rules, the target area is only the trunk and only one fencer may score at a time.

**Foot-work** – mobility, the basic foot and leg movements used during the course of fencing to move forward and backward on the fencing strip, used to attack, defend, and keep distance from your opponent.

**French grip** - a straight type of handle with no finger grips used on foil and epee weapons, often recommended for beginning fencers.

**Guard** – see bell guard

**High line** – the target area above the hip area or above the sword arm when the fencer is in the on-guard position. When the fencer is on-guard with the tip of the weapon higher than the bell, he is said to be "on guard in the high-line".

**Hit** – a hit occurs when the point of the weapon contacts the opponent

**Inside high line**– the shoulder and chest area on the side of unarmed hand

**Inside line** – the area on the unarmed side of the body, on the left side of your blade (for right handed fencers, opposite for left)

**Inside low line** – the area on the unarmed side of the body, below the sword arm or hip area (on the left side of the weapon for right handed fencers)

**Line** – divisions of the target corresponding to the fencing positions. The quadrant of your opponent toward which your blade is pointing.

**Line of attack** – the target area of the opponent at which the point of the weapon of the attacking fencer is directed

**Lines of target** - divide the torso by drawing 2 lines, one vertically from the chin down to the groin, the other horizontally, slightly above the hip. The four sections formed are known as the: the high outside line (6), sword arm shoulder area; the low outside line (8 and 2) on the sword arm side below the bell when in on-guard; the high inside line (4) high chest area, closest to unarmed side; the low inside (7) below bell closest to the unarmed side.

**Low line** – the area below the hip area or the sword arm when in on-guard position. A fencer is on-guard in the low-line when the tip of his weapon is lower than his bell

**Low-line change of engagement** – moving from one side of the opponent's weapon to the other when tips are lower than the bells by moving the tip of your weapon over the top of the opponent's blade, instead of below it. If the opponent disengages your change you will contact the blade on the same side.

**Low-line circle parries** – defensive maneuver done by moving your blade in a circular movement to contact the blade of the attacking opponent when he is attacking you below the hip area.

**Low-line thrust** - a thrust made to the target below the hip (low-line) of the opponent

**Low-line target are**a – the target below the hip area or the area below the sword arm when in on-guard position.

**Lunge** – a type of mobility. From the on-guard position it is a long step done with the front foot. The rear foot and leg pushes and straightens and remains behind in this extended fashion. The purpose is to carry you across a large distance quickly to attack.

**Mobility** – the foot-work or leg movement performed on the fencing strip by the fencers to secure distance from which to attack or defend as well as to repair and maintain the distance during a fencing bout or encounter.

**Modern disengage** – a movement of your blade backward and forward to avoid contact with the opponent's blade who is attempting to contact your blade

**Offense** – aggressive movements done for the purpose of scoring a hit

**On-guard** – to be on-guard is to be in a ready position to move forward or backward as the situation requires, attack or defend in a balanced, well controlled posture.

**On-guard position** - a sideways position that makes you a more difficult target to hit, as well as allowing you a longer reach

**Oppositional parr**y – a defensive blade movement made by contacting the blade of the attacking opponent with your blade and maintaining constant blade contact in order to defend yourself by pushing the opponent's blade aside as you attempt to score a hit.

**Out of distance** – when the distance between you and your opponent is too great for you or your opponent to score.

**Outside high line** – the sword arm shoulder area of a fencer

**Outside line** – the area on the sword arm side of the body

**Outside low line** – the area on the sword arm side of the body below the sword arm when in on-guard, the area below the hip

**Parry** - a defensive maneuver made with the blade to deflect the blade of the attacking opponent away from your target

**Parry 2** – a defensive blade maneuver used to protect the low outside line of your target. It is used to defend against an attack to the rib area in foil, or to the rib, flank, hip, thigh, knee, shin, or foot in epee.

**Parry 4** – a defensive blade maneuver used to protect the high inside target area, your chest area.

**Parry 6** – a defensive blade maneuver used to protect and deflect the blade of the attacking opponent when the attack is directed to your high outside target area (sword arm shoulder area)

**Parry 7** – a defensive blade maneuver used to protect and deflect the blade of the attacking opponent when the attack is directed to your inside low-line

**Parry 8** – a defensive blade maneuver used to protect and deflect the blade of the attack opponent when the attack is directed to the low-outside target (the forward flank or rib area in foil, or to the flank, hip, thigh, knee, shin, or foot in epee)

**Pistol grip** – a type of fencing handle used for foil and epee, an orthopedic style of handle shaped to fit the hand. Developed by a German doctor who had a cripple son that could not hold the French grip.

**Pommel** – a metal nut type device that screws on the blade behind the handle to lock the parts of the weapon together

**Quadrants** – the lines of the target. The four areas that comprise the target area: inside, outside, high, and low

**Recovery** – return to on-guard. The movement following the attack to regain balance and control.

**Right-of-way** – priority given in foil to the opponent that starts the attack or beats the blade last

**Retreat** – backward foot-work used to repair or maintain the distance you desire between you and your opponent

**Riposte** - the action made by the defender to score a touch, after successfully parrying the opponent's attack.

**Salute** – acknowledgement of the referee the audience and the opponent at the beginning and end of every fencing encounter, (bout lesson, drilling session) It shows respect and honor. It is done by bringing the bell to the chin.

**Scoring distance** – distance from which you or your opponent can score a hit.

**Spanking parry** – a defensive blade movement done by crispy beating the blade of the attacking opponent

**Stop thrust** – stop hit – an offensive action made on the opponent's attack

**Straight thrus**t – an offensive action done by moving the point of the weapon to the target by fully extending the sword arm towards the opponent. It is the fastest, easiest, and most effective scoring action.

**Tactics** – the mental analysis necessary to perform the correct fencing action at the right time in the appropriate distance in response to the opponent's action.

**Tempo** – timing, the speed at which fencing actions and maneuvers are made

**Target** – the area on which you deliver the hit with the point or tip of your weapon.

**Thrust** – moving the point of the weapon by the extension of the weapon arm, a forward movement of the blade to make a hit

**Tip** – point or end of the blade or weapon

# ABOUT THE AUTHOR

Having competed in national and international fencing competitions for two decades, Elaine Cheris stands as one of the all-time great U.S. fencers. Also well known as an instructor and administrator, she owns and operates the Cheyenne Fencing and Modern Pentathlon Center, where she has instructed many notable students, including pop music star Jimmy Buffett. She also has been the chairperson for two World Championships (1989 open division, 1993 Under-20 and Under-17) and was the coach of the Junior World Team.

Cheris was the #1 ranked fencer in the United States in 2000 and the highest-ranking American internationally 1998–1999. She is also a three-time Olympian (1980, 1988, 1996), and a member of the 1988 women's foil team that placed sixth in Seoul and the 1996 Atlanta women's epee team that also placed sixth. At the Pan American Games Cheris was a member of the gold-medal women's foil team in 1987 and the gold medal women's epee team in 1991.

She was a member of the U.S. World Championships team in epee six times (1990–1994, 1998) and in foil three times (1982, 1985, 1987).

Cheris graduated from Troy State University in 1970 with a degree in Physical Education/Psychology. She resides in Denver, Colorado.